# THE NAZI YEARS

## A Documentary History

943.086

JOACHIM REMAK, editor of this book, is Professor of History at the University of California, Santa Barbara. He is author of *The Gentle Critic: Theodor Fontane and German Politics* and *Sarajevo: The Story of a Political Murder*, among other books, and is an editor of *Documents on German Foreign Policy, 1918–45*. He has also written numerous articles and reviews for both English- and German-language periodicals.

# THE NAZI YEARS
## A Documentary History

*Edited by*

JOACHIM REMAK

Prentice-Hall, Inc.  *Englewood Cliffs, N.J.*

A SPECTRUM BOOK

Loyalty is the very fire that forever vivifies and sustains the heart of existence.

*Johanna von Puttkamer*
*to her fiancé, Otto von Bismarck*

By the way, the sentence "loyalty is the very fire that forever vivifies and sustains the heart of existence" is one of those nebulous, misty phrases from which it is difficult to derive any clear meaning, and which not infrequently have injurious results when they are carried over from poetry to reality.

*Otto von Bismarck*
*to Johanna von Puttkamer*

My honor is called loyalty.

*Motto of the SS*

# PREFACE

The ideology of National Socialism was vague, eclectic, and change-able. Its practices were unambiguous, often novel, and in fields that af-fected the lives and deaths of millions, pitilessly fixed. But no matter what the degree of clarity, originality, or mutability, it remained true that ideology and practice, theory and fact, were closely connected. Both are described in this volume. They are described by way of documents nearly all of which were written by the actors, victims, or simple wit-nesses of the time and at the time. The form was chosen to lend an immediacy and credibility to the story of the Nazi years which no later writer can quite hope to achieve. And credibility, in this instance, is a special problem, for a generation later, the instinctive reaction to much of Nazi reality is disbelief.

Some of the documents have been published before. Others, notably the political autobiographies of some ordinary Nazi party members, have not. Very few have previously appeared in English. The point is made not to establish any claim to originality, but to point up the basic principle governing the selections. This was to tell, in words not too dulled by familiarity, the whole essential story of National Socialism, from its obscure ideological beginnings to its seizure of power; to show the uses to which that power was put, at home and abroad, until the bitter end of the Third Reich.

There is one other thing worth saying about the documents at this point before they are allowed to speak for themselves. It is an apparent detail, which very much concerns, however, the spirit in which it is hoped this book will be read. All names, even of persons still living, have been given in full, as is of course customary and proper for a his-torical account. Yet there was an occasional temptation to replace a few names with initials, or with an asterisk. For people can make mis-takes, and people can change. (It was a particularly Nazi assumption that the one was impermissible, and the other impossible.) A man who wrote a foolish letter in 1933 or a bloodthirsty editorial in 1939 for what then appeared to him convincing reasons did not thereby commit himself to stupidity or cruelty for the rest of his life. Moreover, this is

being written at a time when it is quite apparent that, while the com-
bination of circumstances that permitted National Socialism to become
a force was clearly unique, many of its individual components were not.
Ideology intoxication, a preference for parading over persuading, intolerance, thinking with one's blood (or nose: "if it smells right it *is*
right"), impatience with the imperfections of democracy, the confusion
of personal truths with schemes for universal salvation, or the veneration
of action for its own sake—all these are both older and younger than
Hitler. "I thank, thee, God, that I am not as other men," said the
Pharisee.

Santa Barbara, California                                            J. R.
September 1968

# CONTENTS

# THE NAZI YEARS

## A Documentary History

# 1

# THE ROOTS

Abandoning these formulae which have but served to give rise to endless errors, we are left with the simple and clear view that our whole civilization and culture of today is the work of one definite race of men—the Teutonic.

> Houston Stewart Chamberlain, *The Foundations of the Nineteenth Century* (1899).

Are you blond? Are you a man? If so, read the Ostara library of those who are blond and support masculine rights.

> Advertisement in Adolf Lanz's *Ostara* (1913).

Many trends, not all of them German, converged to create National Socialism. Most of them were negative in nature: anti-Liberalism, antirationalism, anti-Marxism, antiparliamentarianism, anticlericalism, anti-Semitism. Some were affirmative: an intense nationalism, a cult of the Nordic, a romantic longing for an age both simple and heroic, and, above all, a pseudobiological explanation of the universe derived from Social Darwinism. These individual components of National Socialism— not a few of which contradicted each other—all outdated, by a generation or more, the time when an extraordinary political situation (combined with the display of some extraordinary political talent) allowed Adolf Hitler to assume power in Germany.

Some of the ideas borrowed, Social Darwinism for instance, went through a considerable metamorphosis in Nazi hands. Others, such as the radical anti-Semitism of some late nineteenth-century writers, changed very little. In either case, however, what ought to be said—both in the pursuit of truth and in fairness to authors now dead—is this. To understand the nature of National Socialism, we cannot avoid taking a look at its origins. The history of Nazism does not begin with Hitler's becoming German Chancellor in 1933, or even with the founding of the National Socialist German Workers' Party in Munich in 1919. The roots go deeper. But at the same time, we need to realize that while some of the political and intellectual ancestors of National Socialism would have rejoiced in what they had helped to create (a few, who lived long enough, did just that), others would have been appalled by the abuse of their ideas. Hitler, in other words, read H. S. Chamberlain, and Jules Verne, and some of the other people cited in these pages; they did not read him. Richard Wagner, for all the more than occasional similarities between his outlook and that of some convinced Nazis, was not the first storm trooper. And Ernst Haeckel, who opens this selection, would no more have joined the Nazi Party than Hegel would have joined the First International.

## SOCIAL DARWINISM: ALL LIFE AS A STRUGGLE

Few nineteenth-century books have been as influential as Charles Darwin's *Origin of Species*. It revolutionized not only its own specific field of biology, but was used by admirers of Darwin to explain a variety of social and historical phenomena as well. According to the Social Darwinians, all sorts of groups—nations, races, cultures—were subject to the same laws of natural selection as plants and animals, subject to the same perpetual struggle for existence, the same survival of the stronger, the same elimination of the less fit.

In the beginning, a fair amount of optimism still suffused the thought of people such as Huxley or Spencer. "Pervading all nature," reads what is perhaps the single most famous passage in Herbert Spencer's *Social Statics*, "we may see a stern discipline which is a little cruel that it may be very kind. That state of universal warfare maintained throughout the lower creation, to the great perplexity of many worthy people, is at bottom the most merciful provision which the circumstances admit of."

The optimism is more muted in the leading German exponent of Social Darwinism, Ernst Haeckel. Haeckel (1834–1919), biologist and philosopher, was an immensely popular writer. One of his central theses, briefly alluded to in the passage cited, too, was that of "monism"—the denial of any true distinction between mind and matter, body and spirit; and the postulation of but one single, scientifically ascertainable substance in the world. But other ideas of his did not quite reflect the same mood of rationalist confidence.

There were, the note of caution is worth reiterating, few future gauleiters among Haeckel's readers. In fact, a majority of Nazis would undoubtedly have been embarrassed for an answer had they been asked to define the term Social Darwinism. But among those who did read Haeckel was the young Adolf Hitler, who would select precisely what he wanted from Social Darwinist thought.

> . . . A new and fruitful period of higher development dawned for psychology and all other biological sciences when Charles Darwin, forty years ago, applied to them the principles of the theory of evolution. The seventh chapter of his epoch-making work on the Origin of Species (1859) is devoted to instinct. It combines the valuable proof that the instincts of animals, like all other vital processes, are subject to the general laws of historical development. The special instincts of individual species are formed by adaptation, and their "acquired modifications" are passed on to future generations by heredity; in their formation and development natural selection, by way of the "struggle for existence," plays the same role that it does in transforming any other physiological function. Later, Darwin developed this fundamental thought further in several works, showing that the same laws of "mental evolution" apply throughout the entire organic world, to man as to animals, to animals as to plants.
>
> . . . In the philosophy of history—that is, in the general reflections which historians make on the destinies of nations and the convoluted paths of political evolution—there still prevails the notion of a "moral order of the universe." Historians seek, in the vivid drama of the ups and downs of nations, a leading design, an ideal purpose, which has ordained one state or the other, one race or the other, to prosper and to rule over others. This teleological view of history has recently stood out in even sharper contrast to our monistic view, especially as monism has proved to be the only possible interpretation of all inorganic nature. In astronomy and geology, in the vast field of physics and chemistry, nobody today speaks any longer of a "moral order," or of a personal God, whose "hand hath disposed all things in wisdom and understanding." The same applies to the whole field of biology, to all organic nature. (If we except, for the time being, man himself.) Darwin, by his theory of selection, has shown us not only that the orderly processes in the life and structure of animals and plants have arisen mechanically without any preconceived design, but he has taught us to recognize, in the "struggle for existence," the powerful force of nature, which, for millions of years, has exerted supreme and uninterrupted control over the entire course of the world's organic evolution. Now one can say of

course that the struggle for existence is the "survival of the fittest" or the "victory of the best," but one can do that only if one assumes that the fittest are necessarily, and in a moral sense, the best. Moreover, the entire history of the organic world goes to prove that side by side with great progress toward perfection, we find, at all times, instances of decline toward lower stages. . . .

Is the history of nations—which man, in his anthropocentric megalomania, loves to call "world history"—any different? Do we find in every phase of it a lofty moral principle or a wise ruler, guiding the destiny of nations? There can, in the advanced stage of natural and national history in which we find ourselves today, be only one objective answer to that: No! The fate of those branches of the human family which, as nations and races, have struggled for survival and progress for millennia now, is governed by the same external, iron laws that have determined the history of the entire organic world which for many millions of years has provided life on earth.

. . . [And] the theory of selection teaches us that organic progress is an inevitable consequence of the struggle for existence. Thousands of good and beautiful and admirable species of animals and plants have perished during those forty-eight million years, because they had to make room for other and stronger species, and the victors in this struggle for life were not always the nobler or morally more perfect forms. Precisely the same applies to the history of nations. . . .

> Ernst Haeckel, *Die Welträthsel* (Bonn, 1900), pp. 121 and 311–14. The translation partly follows that of Joseph McCabe, *The Riddle of the Universe at the Close of the Nineteenth Century* (New York, 1900), pp. 104 and 269–71.

## H. S. CHAMBERLAIN: "THE TEUTON IS THE SOUL OF OUR CULTURE"

If the idea of life as a perpetual battle derived from Darwin, that of identifying the superior race with the Germanic, Nordic, Teutonic, or Aryan—the terms are vague and interchangeable and very un-Darwinian—went back to a number of late nineteenth-century writers, each with a special group of disciples of his own. There were Wilhelm Marr and Paul de Lagarde, Eugen Dühring and August Rohling, Theodor Fritsch and a variety of other sectarians, none of whom would probably be remembered today had it not been for their influence on the Nazi movement. Relatively the most influential among them was Houston Stewart Chamberlain (1855–1927), an Englishman who married a daughter of Richard

Wagner, and took up residence in Germany. There he published, in 1899, a book entitled *Die Grundlagen des Neunzehnten Jahrhunderts* (*The Foundations of the Nineteenth Century*), from which the following selection is taken. It was an ambitious and very erudite reinterpretation of history, in which he tried to show that of the three major strains of mankind, two, the Greeks and Romans, had been Aryan and culture-creating, whereas the third had been Semitic and culture-destroying. In 1926, Joseph Goebbels met a very old and ill Chamberlain in Bayreuth, "resting on a chaise, stammering," and called him "father of our spirit, trailblazer, pathmaker." Hitler's basic enthusiasm was equally pronounced, although he made the reservation that Chamberlain had erred in one detail, which was that of considering Christianity an Aryan force.

> . . . *The entrance of the Jew into European history had, as Herder said, meant the entrance of an alien element—alien to that which Europe had already achieved, alien to all it was still destined to achieve. The very reverse was true of the Teuton. This barbarian, who would rush naked to battle, this savage, who suddenly sprang out of woods and marshes to inspire into a world of civilization and culture the terrors of violent conquest won by brute strength alone, is nonetheless the lawful heir to the Hellene and the Roman, blood of their blood and spirit of their spirit. It was his own property which, unwittingly, he snatched from the alien hand. But for him, the sun of the Indo-European would have set. The Asiatic and African slave had, by cowardly murder, wormed his way to the very throne of the Roman Empire; the Syrian mongrel had made himself master of the law; the Jew was using the library at Alexandria to adapt Hellenic philosophy to the Mosaic law; the Egyptian was embalming and burying, for untold ages to come, the fresh and vital bloom of natural science in the ostentatious pyramids of scientific systematization. Soon, too, the sublime flowers of quintessential Aryan life—Indian thought, Indian poetry—were to be trodden underfoot by the savage and bloodthirsty Mongolian; and the desert-maddened Bedouin was to reduce to an everlasting wilderness that garden of Eden, Iran, in which for centuries all the symbolism of the world had grown. Art had long since vanished; in its stead, there were nothing but copies for the rich and circuses for the poor. Thus, to use that expression of Schiller's which I quoted at the beginning of the first chapter, there were no longer men but only creatures. It was high time for the savior to appear. Now he did not enter history in the form which speculative, abstract reason, had it been asked for its advice, would have chosen for a rescuing angel, for the creator of a new dawn of man. But today, when a glance back over the centuries easily teaches us wisdom, we have only one thing to regret. This is that the Teuton did not destroy with more thoroughness wherever his victorious arm reached, and that in consequence the so-called "Latinization," that is the mar-*

riage with the chaos of nations, once more gradually robbed wide regions of the vitalizing influence of pure blood and unbroken youthful vigor, and at the same time deprived them of being ruled by the highest talent. Certainly it can only be shameful indolence of thought or disgraceful historical falsehood which will fail to see, in the entrance of the Germanic tribes into world history, anything but the rescue of a tortured mankind from the claws of the eternally bestial.

. . . When, in this book, I say "Teuton," I mean the various North European races which appear in history as Celts, Teutons, and Slavs, and from which, in irreversible intermingling, the nations of modern Europe are descended. That they originally belonged to a single family is certain; I shall prove it in Chapter Six. However, the Teuton, in the strict Tacitean sense of the term, has proved himself so superior among his kinsmen intellectually, morally, and physically, that we are justified in letting his name serve as the quintessence of the entire family. The Teuton is the soul of our culture. Today's Europe, with its many branches that stretch over the whole globe, is the chequered result of an infinitely manifold mingling of races; what binds us all together and makes an organic unity of us is our Germanic blood. If we look around us today, we see that the importance of each nation as a living power is proportionate to the amount of truly Teutonic blood among its population. Only Teutons sit on the thrones of Europe.

What came earlier in world history, to us are but prolegomena. True history, that history which controls the rhythm of our hearts and pulses through our veins, inspiring us to hope and to creation, begins at that moment when the Teuton seizes the legacy of antiquity with his masterful hand. . . .

> Houston Stewart Chamberlain, *Die Grundlagen des Neunzehnten Jahrhunderts* (Third edition, Munich, 1901), I, 463–64 and 259–60. The translation largely follows that of John Lees, *Foundations of the Nineteenth Century* (New York, 1913), I, 494–95 and 257.

## ANTI-SEMITISM: "IT'S HIS RACE THAT MAKES HIM SUCH A PIG"

The antipode to the masterful Teuton was of course the Jew. Anti-Semitism was not a new phenomenon. What now distinguished it, however, were two things. One was that at a time when the anti-Semitic battle was actually being lost—for the trend in nineteenth-century

Germany was toward full civic rights, and toward the cultural and even the social integration of the Jews—anti-Semitic agitation on the fringes of society was growing ever shriller. The other was that the attacks were based on race and not religion. In earlier periods, conversion to Christianity had always been an available escape from persecution or discrimination. The new anti-Semites would have no part of that. Descent, they held, was far more important than membership in church or synagogue. "*Aus der Rasse kann man nicht austreten*"—"You cannot resign from your race," was the way Georg von Schönerer (1842–1921) put it.

It is from Schönerer, too, from a speech he gave in the Vienna parliament in 1887, that the first selection below is taken. Schönerer was the leader of Austria's small but vocal Pan-German movement, a group that was anti-Habsburg and anti-Roman Catholic as well as anti-Semitic. Hitler would have some kind words for Schönerer in *Mein Kampf*. The second selection, more often quoted than the first, comes from an anonymous follower of his. It was, as a sympathetic biographer put it, a "rougher and more popular version" of Schönerer's basic principles. The third is by a German, rather than an Austrian, pioneer of racial anti-Semitism, Theodor Fritsch (1852–1933) and deals with a frequently advanced counterargument to the new bigotry.

> . . . *It is pure madness to attack the Jews solely because of their faith. Whoever claims that we are fighting the Jews because of their religion is one of those miserable people who is accustomed to defend every other faith and every other nationality and forever to forget his own nation. Our anti-Semitism is not directed against the Jews' religion. It is directed against their racial characteristics, which have changed neither under former pressure nor under the present freedom. On the contrary, the Jews, since their emancipation, have shown themselves more arrogant, hard-hearted, exploitation-minded, and malicious than ever before. There is no place where we do not see them battle the existing order; everywhere they are in league with the forces of rebellion. And it is remarkable that this applies even in those countries where they have achieved an amazingly rapid state of material prosperity. Our racial anti-Semitism thus is not the result of religious intolerance. Rather, it is the indisputable evidence of a nation's new strength and self-confidence, the firm display of national feeling. Therefore, let me repeat this, every loyal son of his nation must see in anti-Semitism the greatest national progress of this century. . . .*

Speech of April 28, 1887; Eduard Pichl, *Georg Schönerer* (Oldenburg, 1938), III, 337–38.

Was der Jude glaubt, ist einerlei—
In der Rasse liegt die Schweinerei!

*What the Jew believes, who cares a fig—*
*It's his race that makes him such a pig!*

> Quoted in Rudolf von Elmayer-Vesten-
> brugg, *Georg Ritter von Schönerer* (Mu-
> nich, 1942), p. 61.

## Did Not Spinoza, Mendelssohn, and Heine Produce Some Important Works?

The fame of the three Jewish celebrities, too, has been very much inflated by Jewish advertising. If they had never lived, nothing essential would be missing from German art and science.

Besides, it is characteristic of these three that they more or less turned away from Judaism, and showed a few better features, which would seem to confirm the suspicion that they were not of purely Jewish blood. Thus, whatever is to be appreciated about them may possibly be due to a few drops of alien blood.

We know that the Jews had so little sympathy for Spinoza's philosophical thoughts that they attempted to do away with the lonely philosopher by excommunication and murder.

In Heine, two forces are noticeably fighting each other. It is as though a piece of Teutonic spirit within him is attempting to ascend to more ideal heights, until the Jew suddenly pulls him down again by the legs into the morass, where he then wallows with delight and jeers at all ideals.

> Theodor Fritsch, *Antisemiten-Katechismus*
> (Leipzig, 1893), pp. 27–28.

## ANTI-SEMITISM: THE JEW AS GRAND CONSPIRATOR

With a certain disregard for logic, broadsides against the Jews' racial inferiority were supplemented by exposés of the Jewish minority's all but successful plots to subvert and dominate the Aryan majority. Among the most determined of these pamphleteers was Adolf Lanz (1874–1954), who usually wrote under the more euphonious and aristocratic name of Georg, or Jörg, Lanz von Liebenfels. Like Schönerer—and Hitler—Lanz was a citizen of the Austro-Hungarian monarchy, and quite generally, it was in Austria rather than in Germany that the roots of National Socialism grew best. (Both extremes, of course, were present in the Habsburg empire: the opportunity for social advancement, on the one hand—more Jews were elevated to the nobility in Vienna than in Berlin—and the existence of a particularly virulent anti-Semitism on the other.) Lanz had his own periodical, the *Ostara*, in which he proclaimed a "heroic biology" and instructed his readers on how they might grade themselves racially. Blue or light grey eyes, for instance, meant twelve plus points on Lanz's scale; dark grey or brown eyes zero, and black eyes twelve minus points. Height, color of skin and hair, shape of the nose, and other physical characteristics could be similarly graded. Possession of 100 plus points identified the bearer as the ideal "Aryo-heroic" type. Men (women were not eligible for the test) with a score above zero but below 100 were "mixed breeds," though with "dominant Aryo-heroic blood"; those below zero were "apelings." Lowest on the scale were the owners of 100 minus points whom Lanz, in an apparent contraction of chimpanzee and vandal, called "chandals." The following table of contents of a 1913 issue of *Ostara* may give some idea of Lanz's ideas and approach:

# Are You Blond? If So, You Are A Culture-Creator and Culture-Supporter!

## Therefore Read the "Ostara" Library of Those Who Are Blond and Support Masculine Rights!

### No. 72
### Race and Foreign Policy
#### by J. Lanz-Liebenfels

Contents: Racial-psychological and racial-historical foundations of policy; the racial classification of various nations and states; the cosmopolitanism of the blond and the mendacious policies of the dark races; mongoloid "realistic" and "social" policy; Mediterranean universal policy; Jewish and Jesuit world power; the program of the Alliance israélite; racial affinities between Jews and Jesuits; Austro-German policy; the Triple Alliance as the guarantor of the emancipation of the Jews and the continued existence of the Jesuit order; trouble in the Triple Alliance?; the financial, literary, and political boycott of anti-Semitic German-Austrians by the Alliance; Albania and the Balkans—problems not for Austria but for Berlin, Budapest, and Rome; the splendid future of an Austria-Hungary purged and unified in an Aryo-Christian spirit; the collapse of the chandalistic world policy; an Austro-British alliance as the turning point in an Aryo-Christian world policy.

Two illustrations: The Jewish and Jesuit Popes as representatives of anti-Aryan
world policy.

Publisher: "Ostara," Mödling-Vienna, 1913.

> Quoted in Wilfried Daim, *Der Mann der
> Hitler die Ideen gab* (Munich, 1958), p.
> 145.

## PAN-GERMANISM: THE GREATER
## GERMANIC EMPIRE

Anti-Semitism, as noted, constituted only one part of Schönerer's Pan-German program. Equally important were anti-Catholicism and a territorial program that demanded the abandonment of the Habsburg empire's non-German lands, the union of German-speaking Austria with the new German Reich, and the establishment of a Greater Teutonic Empire. The precise borders of such an empire were not defined too clearly, but at one point Schönerer thought that it should include the Boer Republic.

The first selection is the Pan-German program of 1913, a briefer version of a program first formulated in 1895. The second is its even shorter summing up, in the verse form favored by Schönerer in his Pan-German propaganda.

## *The Grand Pan-German Aim:*

*The establishment of a unitary state, independent toward all sides, and including all Germans of Central Europe. The basis of the state to be Aryan, the language German, the law German, and science to be free. Its citizens to be tied together by a single faith, free of Rome and free of dogma. A unitary state that is to be the center of all German life on this globe, to be connected with all Teutonic states.*

> Heinrich Schnee, *Georg Ritter von Schö-
> nerer* (Reichenberg, 1943), p. 186.

Ohne Juda, ohne Rom
Wird gebaut Germaniens Dom!

*Without Juda, without Rome
We shall build our German Dom!*

> Elmayer-Vestenbrugg, *Schönerer*, p. 87.

## PAN-GERMANISM: PREINDUSTRIAL LONGINGS

At about the same time that Schönerer was active in Vienna, a Pan-German group was being formed in Berlin. Its leader was a lawyer, Heinrich Class (1868–1953). The two groups were independent of each other, and on some points their views differed. Class, for instance, had no particular desire for Austro-German union, and his anti-Semitism, although equally racial in nature, tended to be a shade less fanatical than Schönerer's. (Some occasional German Jews, Class thought, were decent people.) Where the two groups were very much in harmony, however, was in mood. Both were aggressively Teutonic and expansionist. Both, too, were antimodern in temper, vaguely anticapitalist as well as definitely anti-Marxist. They were nostalgic for an earlier age in which life, they felt, had been simpler, more honest, and less hectic.

The first selection is from *If I Were Emperor*, a very successful book Class published in 1912 under the pseudonym of Daniel Fryman, in which he developed his Pan-German program at some length. It has been chosen not so much for its anti-American tone, which was neither a consistent nor a very essential point in Pan-German ideology, as for the anti-industrial, antimaterialist longings to which it gives words.

The second, very much sharper, passage (Class was no primitive who would have destroyed industrial society) is from Lanz's *Ostara*.

### Americanization

We must do some fresh thinking, too, on the inviolability of the concept of laissez-faire, which in too many cases is nothing but a mask covering the most ruthless exploitation of the less fortunate by the momentarily more successful.

We must understand that we are doing great damage to the physical and intellectual strength of our nation, and that if we persist in our present course, premature exhaustion will be the result.

Let me mention in passing only that our nation has been advised to learn from the Americans, to find out from them how to run an economy. As though the Jews in our midst were not teachers enough!

How can anyone possibly appear on our market-places and suggest "Americanization" to us! This most unfeeling form of business behavior, devoid of common decency and of common trust, bare of any social compassion, surely is the way of life of the predatory animal, which could have been produced only by a mish-mash of nations without race and culture.

Some people were sufficiently lacking in instinct to recommend this model to us, while the Jews had instinct enough to comprehend immediately that it would mean new grist for their mills.

Our proud industry, our honorable commerce, will know that unless they are to suffer grievously, the advice must be rejected—all moral considerations quite aside, which, to use the well-worn phrase, are "a matter of course." It is a sad thing that even without the Godless counsel of Americanization, competition has assumed forms which frequently violate the commands of decency and of justice. . . .

> Heinrich Class [Daniel Fryman], *Wenn ich der Kaiser wär* (Second edition, Leipzig, 1912), pp. 128–29.

. . . Only the man who is wedded to the soil, the farmer, is truly a man. . . . Therefore the Aryan race will prosper only amid the culture of the countryside; the city is its grave. . . .

> Adolf Lanz, in *Ostara*, No. 23, 1908; quoted in Daim, *Der Mann*, p. 117.

## ROMANTICISM: THE SEARCH FOR CAMELOT . . .

Preindustrial longings and myth of the soil; there enters, as we look at Nazism's nineteenth-century roots, a strongly irrational element that defies analysis. We might, for lack of a better term, call it popularized romanticism, a more stagy and diffuse version of the original romantic school and mood. Among its best vehicles was the opera, among its most typical spokesmen, Hitler's favorite composer, Richard Wagner.

Again, as in Haeckel's case, the question of historical fairness arises. There is infinitely more to Wagner, obviously, than Hitler's affinity for his music. And why not, instead of Wagner, cite the science fiction of Jules Verne or the splendid Westerns of Karl May, both of whom, too, supplied the age with daydreams, and numbered Hitler among their readers. The answer is that certain terms recur in Wagner which will be found again and again in the Nazi vocabulary; *das Reich*, for instance —a vaguely used term capable of many interpretations: the realm, the medieval empire, or Bismarck's empire, or in fact any empire, a secular kingdom or the kingdom of God. Beside, there is the matter of mood, the quest for grail and *Reich*, the operatic dream:

Chorus. All the Men. (striking on their shields as the King reaches the oak.)

Heil,_____  Kö - nig  Hein - rich!
Hail,_____  roy - al  Hen - ry,

Kö - nig  Hein - rich  Heil!_____
roy - al  Hen - ry,  hail!_____

On the stage.
Tpts. of the King.

All the Tpts. on the stage.  Side Drums (on the stage)
Tpts. in Orch.
dim.

·12946

The King.

Habt  Dank, ihr  Lie - ben von Bra-bant!
Have  thanks, good  lie - ges of Bra-bant!

p  p Tpts. Tromb. & Tb.  cresc.

Sieg! Sieg! Sieg!
Heil dir, Heil!

Victory! Victory! Victory!
Hail to you, Hail!

Hence, listening to the Ring cycle may do as much to illuminate
Nazism's background as any academic inquiry can.

There follow two brief excerpts from Lohengrin. In the first, King
Henry is addressing his knights; in the second, Lohengrin has finally,
and against his will, revealed his true identity to Elsa:

MEN OF BRABANT [beating against their shields]:
Hail King Henry! King Henry, Hail!
    KING:    Good subjects of Brabant, 'tis well
With pride I feel my heart now swell
May I in every German land
Find such a true and loyal band.
Let the Reich's enemy now appear
We're well prepared to see him near.
From his Eastern desert plain
He'll never dare to stir again!
The German sword for German land!
Thus will the Reich in vigor stand!
    MEN OF BRABANT:    The German sword for Germand land!
Thus will the Reich in vigor stand!

. . .
    LOHENGRIN:    In a far country, you will never see it
Rises a castle, Montsalvat by name
There stands a temple, brilliant white forever
So glorious, all on earth is void of fame.
In it, a vessel, wondrous powers possessing
Is guarded as a sacred treasure beyond cost.
That unstained men may keep it as a blessing
'Twas brought to earth by an angelic host.
Once every year a dove, from heaven descending
Alights, and thus its marvelous strength renews.
It's called the Grail. This, to its pure knights lending
Its virtue, does into them a blessed faith infuse.
He whom the Grail to be its servant chooses
It arms with more than earthly might.
Opposed to him, deceit its magic loses
His piercing glance defeats even death's night.
In distant countries too, in his possession
The chosen knight his matchless power retains.
To fight for virtue, to resist oppression—
But only while his name unknown remains.

So pure's the Grail in nature and so holy
That from all common eyes its needs must be concealed.
To doubt its strength is arrogance and folly
Its champions leave, if once their name's reveal'd.
Now hear! Hear how this knight suspicion scorneth!
Sent hither by the Holy Grail, I came,
Its knight. My father now its crown adorneth—
Great Percival. And Lohengrin's my name.

> Richard Wagner, *Lohengrin, Romantische Oper in Drei Akten*, Act 3, Scene 3 (Leipzig, *c.* 1880), pp. 41–44. The translation partly follows that of *Lohengrin, Opera in Three Acts, As Represented at the Royal Italian Opera, London, and at the Academy of Music, New York* (New York, *c.* 1890), pp. 27–29.

## . . . AND LANCELOT

Nor was the quest restricted to the stage. Here are the closing words from Schönerer's last speech:

Pan-Germany is and was my dream.
And I close with a Hail!
To the Bismarck of the future, the savior of the Germans
And the Creator of Pan-Germany
Hail to Bismarck II, Hail to him, a threefold Hail!

> October 18, 1913; Schnee, *Schönerer*, p. 100.

# 2
## THE SOIL

We who love the old German Fatherland recognize the unextinguishable debt which we as individuals, and with us the entire world of civilization, owe to it for the enrichment and liberation of our single lives and of the whole community life of man upon the globe.

> Benjamin Ide Wheeler, "Germany's Place in the Sun," *The Fatherland* (November 18, 1914).

The territories which were ceded to Germany in accordance with . . . the Treaty of Frankfurt of May 10, 1871, are restored to French sovereignty as from the date of the Armistice of November 11, 1918.

By a date which must not be later than March 31, 1920, the German Army must not comprise more than seven divisions of infantry and three divisions of cavalry.

As a guarantee for the execution of the present Treaty by Germany, the German territory situated to the west of the Rhine, together with the bridgeheads, will be occupied by Allied and Associated troops for a period of fifteen years from the coming into force of the present Treaty.

> From Articles 51, 160, and 428 of the Treaty of Versailles (1919).

What drew me to the folkish, and later to the National Socialist movement, was not anything of which I was clearly conscious. My feeling told me: what they want is right, they are putting into words things which you have always sensed to be right and good. It is only if we become fanatics, and put our

*country above everything . . . that we will amount to some-
thing again.*

> From the political autobiography of
> *Obersturmführer* Georg Zeidler,
> 1934.

Wagner, we should remind ourselves, was honored as a great composer, not as an ideological guide. Schönerer and his friends were leading
a movement whose Bismarck veneration went unappreciated by the
subject of its affections. Pre-1914 German, and even Austrian, societies
were strong enough to absorb their various fringe movements. The pre-
dominant mood was expressed in the lines of Viktor von Scheffel, historical novelist and prolific writer of student songs:

> *A toast, a toast to the German Reich! . . .*
> *May daily it be strengthened.*
> *But may God preserve it from class hatred*
> *And race hatred, and mass hatred*
> *And such like works of the devil.*

Or here are the recollections of Benjamin Ide Wheeler (written in
1914, when he was President of the University of California) of a
Germany that led Europe in industrial power, in military strength, and
in the number of Nobel Prize winners:

> *. . . The Germany I knew first was the Germany of the universities.
> I sat on the benches of Leipzig, Jena, Heidelberg, and Berlin and lis-
> tened to the patient unfolding of ordered knowledge from the lips of
> Curtius, Zarncke, Lange and Brugmann at Leipzig; Osthoff, Wachs-
> muth, and the inimitable Kuno Fischer at Heidelberg; Delbrück,
> Haeckel and Kluge at Jena; Scherer, Kirchhoff and Freitschke and
> Schmidt at Berlin; but better, wandered over the hills of Jena and
> Heidelberg, up to the Forst and down the valley of Kunitz, up the
> Neckar, and over the Königstuhl in company with one or another of
> these men, communing by the way over things of the spirit, and learn-
> ing to know from Germany and her men what it means to stand on the
> frontiers of the known, to study at first hand, to think independently,
> and above all, having done this, to teach "with authority"—not the
> authority of a stamped and well-engrossed diploma, but with the author-
> ity of independent knowledge—to "teach with authority and not as the
> scribes." This—which is the real Germany—I saw first, then later the
> Germany of government, law, order, which made the inner life possible.
> Every noon as I left the University of Berlin I saw the "old Emperor"
> standing at his window in the Palace as the guard marched by. Now
> and again I saw the towering figure of Bismarck. At the autumn
> manoeuvres in Hanover I saw the forty or fifty thousand men pass in

*faultless review before a group of three on horseback, the old Emperor, the Crown Prince Frederick, and von Moltke.*

*Very different men in outward guise were these trim soldiers from the bent and tousled professors who first interpreted to me Germany, but I came to find out that each group respected the other, and that both went to make up Germany as the whole. Without the professors it were a hollow thing; without soldier and Emperor, without order and defense, it were feeble and poor, crushed between the two jaws of the vise, Russia and France, the Slav and the Roman.*

*Now within the last four years by the chance of three visits I have renewed, after an interval of a quarter century, my acquaintance with the land and its people. Forty years of peace guaranteed by soldier and government had given full rein to patient industry and scientific orderliness, and brought to high fruitage the alliance of shop and laboratory. . . .*

Benjamin Ide Wheeler, "Germany's Place<br>in the Sun," The Fatherland, I, No. 15<br>(November 18, 1914), 1.

## THE WAR

Some extraordinary things had to happen to destroy this Germany. They did. War, revolution, inflation, and depression created a society that was ready to listen to the kind of prophet so generally ignored before.

The war, the Germans thought, had been fought in an honorable cause, that of the nation's survival "between the two jaws of the vise." The conflict's cost had been staggering; out of a total population of 67 million in 1914, Germany suffered these casualties in World War I:

*. . . The losses in the German army and navy calculated on the basis of the official casualty lists up to no. 1,284 of October 24, 1918, were:*

### GERMAN ARMY AND NAVY CASUALTIES

|         | Killed    | Wounded   | Missing | Total     |
|---------|-----------|-----------|---------|-----------|
| Army    | 1,582,244 | 3,654,175 | 756,843 | 5,993,262 |
| Navy    | 28,860    | 28,968    | 15,679  | 73,507    |
| Total   | 1,611,104 | 3,683,143 | 772,522 | 6,066,769 |

A large proportion of the missing, certainly nine-tenths, must be

reckoned as dead, so that the total number of deaths, according to this
statement, must be put at about 2,300,000.

Samuel Dumas and K. O. Vedel-Peterson,
*Losses of Life Caused by War* (Oxford,
1923), p. 141.

## THE PEACE

Yet when the war was over, and lost, the Germans were told that their
emperor was a criminal, and that they, as a nation, fully deserved the
punitive peace the Allies were imposing on them. Under the terms of
the Treaty of Versailles, the Germans lost every one of their overseas
possessions, and a good deal of German territory as well. They also were
ordered to disarm, and to pay reparations for the war which, they were
informed, they and their allies—and no one else—had started. There
follows the war guilt clause of the Treaty of Versailles, which Hitler, in
his speaking tours of the Twenties, made it a habit to carry with him:

## Article 231

The Allied and Associated Governments affirm and Germany accepts
the responsibility of Germany and her allies for causing all the loss and
damage to which the Allied and Associated Governments and their
nationals have been subjected as a consequence of the war imposed
upon them by the aggression of Germany and her allies.

*Treaty of Peace Between the Allied and
Associated Powers and Germany. Signed at
Versailles, June 28, 1919* (London, 1919),
p. 101.

## REVOLUTION

The government which was made to sign this confession was not that
of the Kaiser. It was that of the German republic which had been proclaimed, by revolution, at the end of 1918. The new government accepted
the victor's peace for the sole reason that it saw no alternative. The new
Social Democratic defense minister told the troops in the summer of
1919 that he had voted for rejecting the treaty, but that "new and
immense sufferings are to be prevented by our submitting to the enemy's
will. Whether the effort will succeed, no one can yet say."

The words were spoken in vain. A host of domestic critics soon
attacked the new republic as the state that had gladly accepted a shame-

ful peace. They created legends such as that of the stab in the back. The
army, they said, had been undefeated in the field; it had been betrayed
at home. The charges were as mendacious as they were effective. And a
charge that was true as well as effective was that, in a country divided by
an issue so basic as loyalty to republic or loyalty to monarchy, parliamentary government worked badly. There were, under the system of
proportional representation adopted by the republic, too many parties to
allow for stability.

Below is a ballot for the Reichstag election of 1930. (The translation
gives the names of the parties only; these are followed in the original
by the names of the leading candidates nominated by each party.) The
other selection is a description of some people's feelings toward the
workings of parliamentary democracy, based on a series of interviews
with a group of ex-Nazis conducted by an American social scientist,
Milton Mayer, in the nineteen-fifties:

## Reichstag Election

### Electoral District of Schleswig-Holstein

1. Social Democratic Party of Germany                                            1
2. German National People's Party                                                2
3. Center Party                                                                  3
4. Communist Party                                                               4
5. German People's Party                                                         5
5a. Christian-Social National Community                                          5a
6. German State Party                                                            6
7. National Party of the German Middle Class (Economic
   Party)                                                                        7
9. National Socialist German Workers' Party (Hitler Move-
   ment)                                                                         9
10. Peasant and Farmfolk Party of Schleswig-Holstein            10
11a. People's Rights Party (National Party for People's Rights
   and Revaluation) and National Christian-Social Party          11a
11b. People's Rights Party                                                       11b
12. German Farmers' Party                                                        12
16. Treviranus-Conservative People's Party                              16
17. Christian-Social National Service                                            17
19a. Polish People's Party                                                       19a
19b. Schleswig League                                                            19b
19c. Friesland                                                                   19c
23. Independent Social Democratic Party of Germany         23
24. Landlords and Real Estate Owners                                    24
28. Party of Mankind and New National Community           28

## Reichstagswahl
### Wahlkreis Schleswig-Holstein

|  |  | | |
|---|---|---|---|
| 1 | **Sozialdemokratische Partei Deutschlands** <br> Schroeder, Luiſe — Eggerſtedt — Richter — Bieſter | 1 | ◯ |
| 2 | **Deutſchnationale Volkspartei** <br> Oberfohren — Gerns — Wülfing von Ditten — Goth | 2 | ◯ |
| 3 | **Zentrum** <br> Brüning — Häfner — Fuchs, Hedwig — Germeshauſen | 3 | ◯ |
| 4 | **Kommuniſtiſche Partei** <br> Thälmann — Auguſtat, Eliſe — Heuck — Röhrs | 4 | ◯ |
| 5 | **Deutſche Volkspartei** <br> Dr. Schifferer — Fiſcher — Cimbal, Eliſabeth — Helms | 5 | ◯ |
| 5a | **Chriſtlich-ſoziale Volksgemeinſchaft** <br> Broderſen — Grohinger — Wagner | 5a | ◯ |
| 6 | **Deutſche Staatspartei** <br> Paulſen — Dr. Kiep-Altenloh, Emilie — Apfeld Ohlrogge | 6 | ◯ |
| 7 | **Reichspartei des Deutſchen Mittelſtandes (Wirtſchaftspartei)** <br> Köſter — Reimers — Musfeldt — Kähler | 7 | ◯ |
| 9 | **Nationalſozialiſtiſche Deutſche Arbeiterpartei (Hitlerbewegung)** <br> Franzen — Meyer-Quade — Thormählen — Stamer | 9 | ◯ |
| 10 | **Bauern- u. Landvolkpartei Schleswig-Holſtein** <br> (Chriſtlich-Nationale Bauern- und Landvolkpartei) <br> Schiele — Kähler — Mangelſen — Behrens | 10 | ◯ |
| 11a | **Volksrechtpartei (Reichspartei für Volksrecht und Aufwertung) und Chriſtlich-Soziale Reichspartei** <br> Graf Poſadowsky-Wehner—Fleck—Henniger—Kuſchert | 11a | ◯ |
| 11b | **Volksrechtpartei** <br> Merts — Mohr — Richter — Roeſchel · | 11b | ◯ |
| 12 | **Deutſche Bauernpartei** <br> Leu — Wulff — Harenberg — Gößler | 12 | ◯ |
| 16 | **Treviranus-Konſervative Volkspartei** <br> Treviranus — Lambach — Rieger — von Uhlefeld | 16 | ◯ |
| 17 | **Chriſtlich-ſozialer Volksdienſt** <br> Matthieſen — Thieſen — Büntjen — Stolze | 17 | ◯ |
| 19a | **Polniſche Volkspartei** <br> Ledvolorz — Latuniezak — Zydor — Kivleiniewſki | 19a | ◯ |
| 19b | **Schleswigſcher Verein** <br> Gdgaard — Peterſen — Jper — Laſſen | 19b | ◯ |
| 19c | **Friesland** <br> Olßen — Henningſen — Peterſen — Lorenzen | 19c | ◯ |
| 23 | **Unabhängige Sozialdemokratiſche Partei Deutſchlands** <br> Liebknecht — Wiegmann, Elſa — Helder — Schröder | 23 | ◯ |
| 24 | **Haus- und Grundbeſitzer** <br> Wehner — Kohlmorgen — Krabad — Schramm | 24 | ◯ |
| 28 | **Menſchheitspartei und Neue Volksgemeinſchaft** <br> Heydorn — Reimpell — Thiel — Duus | 28 | ◯ |

George Soldan, ed., *Zeitgeschichte in Wort und Bild* (Oldenburg, 1934), III, 333.

. . . National Socialism was a revulsion by my friends against parliamentary politics, parliamentary debate, parliamentary government—
against all the higgling and the haggling of the parties and the splinter
parties, their coalitions, their confusions, and their conniving. It was
the final fruit of the common man's repudiation of "the rascals." Its
motif was, "Throw them all out." My friends, in the 1920's, were like
spectators at a wrestling match who suspect that beneath all the grunts
and groans, the struggle and the sweat, the match is "fixed," that the
performers are only pretending to put on a fight. The scandals that
rocked the country, as one party or cabal "exposed" another, dis-
mayed and then disgusted my friends. . . .

Milton Mayer, *They Thought They Were
Free* (Chicago, 1955), p. 101.

## INFLATION AND DEPRESSION

Quite possibly, of course, no government could have coped with the
problems that faced Germany in the Twenties. For soon after the war
came an inflation that destroyed much of the middle class. It was
followed, six years later, by a depression of unprecedented severity.

The note on the inflation (during its more moderate phase, the price
of bread rose to 2500 marks, and an egg cost 800 marks) comes from the
diary of Lord D'Abernon, the British ambassador to Berlin. The figures
on unemployment and business failures, which begin with the last
"normal" year of 1928, have been compiled from the German statistical
yearbook.

Berlin, August 11, 1922.—One of the comedy-tragedy episodes of
the visit of the Committee of Guarantees to Berlin was the payment by
the German Government of their railway expenses, including their
special car, which waited here six weeks. This was done in 20-mark
notes, and it required seven office boys with huge waste-paper-baskets
full of these notes to carry the full sum from the office down to the
railway station. . . .

An Ambassador of Peace, Lord D'Abernon's Diary (London, 1929–1930), II, 81.

UNEMPLOYMENT IN GERMANY, 1928–1932[1]

| Year | Number |
|------|-----------|
| 1928 | 1,862,000 |
| 1929 | 2,850,000 |
| 1930 | 3,217,000 |
| 1931 | 4,886,000 |
| 1932 | 6,042,000 |

Manuel Saitzew, ed., *Die Arbeitslosigkeit der Gegenwart* (Munich, 1932), p. 151; and *Statistisches Jahrbuch für das Deutsche Reich, 1933* (Berlin, 1934), p. 291.

BANKRUPTCIES IN GERMANY, 1928–1932

| Year | Number |
|------|--------|
| 1928 | 10,595 |
| 1929 | 13,180 |
| 1930 | 15,486 |
| 1931 | 19,254 |
| 1932 | 14,138 |

*Statistisches Jahrbuch*, 1929, p. 354; 1930, p. 398; 1931, p. 378; 1932, p. 374; 1933, p. 384.

# A WAY OUT?

It was in this soil that the Nazi movement—or to give it its formal name, the National Socialist German Workers' Party—grew and prospered. It was against this background that an Austrian immigrant to Germany, who had been denied admission to Vienna's school of architecture, and who had been unable to decide on a career for himself ever since, discovered that he possessed a very great talent, that of public speaking.

[1] The figures apply to the end of January of each year, when unemployment tended to be at its highest level. Even so, however, the actual picture was somewhat worse than here indicated, since the figures include only "the unemployed registered with labor offices."

The three documents that follow give some idea of one of Nazism's most important roots—Hitler's ability to sway a crowd. The first dates from the year 1919. Adolf Hitler, born in Austria in 1889, but a resident of Munich since 1913, had volunteered for army duty as soon as the war broke out. For four years, he served with considerable bravery, although he did not rise above the rank of corporal. In 1919, he was hired by the German army command in Munich as a combined intelligence and education officer, and the excerpt printed conveys the impressions of another army member, sent to report on his performance. The second selection records the observations of a visitor to an election meeting in Hamburg in 1927. The third, written in 1934, is taken from the political autobiography of a storm troop lieutenant. It was collected, along with some 600 other such biographies, by an American sociologist, Theodore Abel. In 1934, Abel went to Germany, where, with some cooperation from party authorities, he invited people who had joined the Nazi movement prior to its accession of power in 1933 to indicate what had prompted them to do so. (Professor Abel summed up his evaluations of these autobiographies in a book, *Why Hitler Came to Power,* and presented the original manuscripts to the Hoover Institution on War, Revolution, and Peace, at Stanford, Calif., where they now remain.)

. . . *"All's well that ends well,"* I'd say here, for I am surprised and delighted by the successes which our education squad has achieved in these five days. The lion's share of the success no doubt belongs to Herr Hitler and Herr Beyschlag, who were able, by their splendid speeches, to attract the attention, and the interest, of the company. . . . Herr Hitler, if I might put it this way, is the born popular speaker, and by his fanaticism and his crowd appeal he clearly attracts the attention of the audience, and compels it to share his trend of thought. . . .

> Report of Lorenz Frank to Army Group Command No. 4, in Werner Maser, *Die Frühgeschichte der NSDAP* (Frankfurt, 1965), p. 139.

. . . *How did Hitler cast a spell over his listeners?* In the faces of the storm troopers who were guarding the hall you saw a vain effort to follow the details of what the speaker was saying. But their faces did not relax. What they heard in his words was something that, without having created any intellectual concepts, will emerge in some street battle when they will defend their swastika. . . .

> Albrecht Erich Günther, "Hitler," *Deutsches Volkstum* (December 1927), in Werner Jochmann, *Nationalsozialismus und Revolution* (Frankfurt, 1963), p. 271.

. . . We old National Socialists did not join the storm troops from any rational considerations, or after much contemplation. It was our feelings that led us to Hitler. What we felt, what our hearts compelled us to think, was this—Hitler, you're our man. You talk like a human being who's been at the front, who's been through the same mess we were, and not in some soft berth, but like us as an unknown soldier. You are pleading, with all your being, with all your burning heart, for us, the Germans. You want what is best for Germany not because it will benefit you personally; no, it is because you can do no other, because this is the way you must act out of your most profound convictions as a man of decency and of honor. He who once looked into Hitler's eyes, he who once heard him, will never get away from him again. . . .

Autobiography of *Obersturmführer* Georg Zeidler, August 30, 1934. (Ms. in the Abel collection of the Hoover Institution on War, Revolution, and Peace, Stanford, California)

# 3

## THE PROGRAM

*We demand the creation and support of a healthy middle class, and the immediate socialization of the huge department stores, and their lease, at low rates, to small tradesmen. . . .*

> From the program of the National Socialist German Workers' Party (1920).

*The race question is the key not only to world history but to human culture itself.*

> Adolf Hitler, *Mein Kampf* (1924).

## "COMMON INTEREST BEFORE SELF-INTEREST": THE PROGRAM

The party to which Hitler decided to give his talents (he had become acquainted with it by attending its meetings as part of his work for the army) was not appreciably different from a number of other right wing, or "folkish" groups. The National Socialist German Workers' Party had been founded in Munich in 1919. It was opposed to Versailles and Communism and defeat and Jews and pacifism and parliamentary democracy. It believed in the German folk soul—the term *"völkisch,"* which it was fond of using, is as elusive as "folkish" or "folk soul" are in English—and had strongly socialist and vaguely authoritarian leanings. Its official

27

780958

program, proclaimed in 1920, was wide-ranging and confused enough to let the party appear as less than a major threat to the existing order:

## Program of the National Socialist German Workers' Party

The Program of the German Workers' Party is a limited program. Its leaders have no intention, once its aims have been achieved, of establishing new ones, merely in order to insure the continued existence of the party by the artificial creations of discontent among the masses.

1. We demand, on the basis of the right of national self-determination, the union of all Germans in a Greater Germany.

2. We demand equality for the German nation among other nations, and the revocation of the peace treaties of Versailles and Saint-Germain.

3. We demand land (colonies) to feed our people and to settle our excess population.

4. Only a racial comrade can be a citizen. Only a person of German blood, irrespective of religious denomination, can be a racial comrade. No Jew, therefore, can be a racial comrade.

5. Noncitizens shall be able to live in Germany as guests only, and must be placed under alien legislation.

6. We therefore demand that every public office, no matter of what kind, and no matter whether it be national, state, or local office, be held by none but citizens.

We oppose the corrupting parliamentary custom of making party considerations, and not character and ability, the criterion for appointments to official positions.

7. We demand that the state make it its primary duty to provide a livelihood for its citizens. If it should prove impossible to feed the entire population, the members of foreign nations (noncitizens) are to be expelled from Germany.

8. Any further immigration of non-Germans is to be prevented. We demand that all non-Germans who entered Germany after August 2, 1914, be forced to leave the Reich without delay.

9. All citizens are to possess equal rights and obligations.

10. It must be the first duty of every citizen to perform mental or physical work. Individual activity must not violate the general interest, but must be exercised within the framework of the community, and for the general good.

THEREFORE WE DEMAND:

*11. The abolition of all income unearned by work and trouble.*

## BREAK THE SLAVERY OF INTEREST

*12.* In view of the tremendous sacrifices of life and property imposed by any war on the nation, personal gain from the war must be characterized as a crime against the nation. We therefore demand the total confiscation of all war profits.

*13.* We demand the nationalization of all business enterprises that have been organized into corporations (trusts).

*14.* We demand profit-sharing in large industrial enterprises.

*15.* We demand the generous development of old age insurance.

*16.* We demand the creation and support of a healthy middle class, and the immediate socialization of the huge department stores and their lease, at low rates, to small tradesmen. We demand that as far as national, state, or municipal purchases are concerned, the utmost consideration be shown to small tradesmen.

*17.* We demand a land reform suitable to our national needs, and the creation of a law for the expropriation without compensation of land for communal purposes. We demand the abolition of ground rent, and the prohibition of all speculation in land.

*18.* We demand a ruthless battle against those who, by their activities, injure the general good. Common criminals, usurers, profiteers, etc., are to be punished by death, regardless of faith or race.

*19.* We demand that Roman law, which serves a materialist world order, be replaced by German law.

*20.* To open the doors of higher education—and thus to leading positions—to every able and hard-working German, the state must provide for a thorough restructuring of our entire educational system. The curricula of all educational institutions are to be brought into line with the requirements of practical life. As soon as the mind begins to develop, the schools must teach civic thought (citizenship classes). We demand the education, at state expense, of particularly talented children of poor parents, regardless of the latters' class or occupation.

*21.* The state must see to it that national health standards are raised. It must do so by protecting mothers and children, by prohibiting child labor, by promoting physical strength through legislation providing for compulsory gymnastics and sports, and by the greatest possible support for all organizations engaged in the physical training of youth.

*22.* We demand the abolition of the mercenary army and the creation of a people's army.

23. We demand legal warfare against intentional political lies and their dissemination through the press. To facilitate the creation of a German press, we demand:

(a) that all editors of, and contributors to, newspapers that appear in the German language be racial comrades;

(b) that no non-German newspaper may appear without the express permission of the government. Such papers may not be printed in the German language;

(c) that non-Germans shall be forbidden by law to hold any financial share in a German newspaper, or to influence it in any way.

We demand that the penalty for violating such a law shall be the closing of the newspapers involved, and the immediate expulsion of the non-Germans involved.

Newspapers which violate the general good are to be banned. We demand legal warfare against those tendencies in art and literature which exert an undermining influence on our national life, and the suppression of cultural events which violate this demand.

24. We demand freedom for all religious denominations, provided they do not endanger the existence of the state, or violate the moral and ethical feelings of the Germanic race.

The party, as such, stands for positive Christianity, without, however, allying itself to any particular denomination. It combats the Jewish-materialistic spirit within and around us, and is convinced that a permanent recovery of our people can be achieved only from within, on the basis of

## THE COMMON INTEREST BEFORE SELF-INTEREST

25. To implement all these points, we demand the creation of a strong central power in Germany. A central political parliament should possess unconditional authority over the entire Reich, and its organization in general.

Corporations based on estate and profession should be formed to apply the general legislation passed by that Reich in the various German states.

The leaders of the party promise to do everything that is in their power, and if need be, to risk their very lives, to translate this program into action.

Munich, February 24, 1920.

Gottfried Feder, *Das Programm der N.S.D.A.P. und seine weltanschaulichen Grundgedanken* (Munich, 1932), pp. 19–22.

## AUTHORITY AND RACE: HITLER AND
## THE PARTY PROGRAM

What Hitler did with this program was to de-emphasize its socialist part—not to the point of driving away the dispossessed, but to that of not antagonizing the potential middle-class sympathizer. (Even before Hitler came to dominate the party, of course, its socialism had been a great deal closer to American populism than to Marxist socialism; it was "break the slavery of interest," not "proletarians of all countries unite.") On the other hand, he very much emphasized the party's antiparliamentary mood, and offered, in place of the democratic system, his "Führerprinzip," or the utter authority of the leader. What he also retained, and emphasized time and again, was the supernationalist mood of the party.

Both quotations are from *Mein Kampf*, written in prison in 1924, after Hitler's attempt, the previous year, to achieve power by revolutionary means had failed. The first is self-explanatory; the second follows upon a passage in which he explained how Germany had lost the war because it had failed to realize that the true enemy—Marxists, pacifists, Jews— resided within its own borders.

. . . *In big things and in small, the movement advocates the principle of the unconditional authority of the leader, coupled with the greatest responsibility.. . . .*

*It is one of the supreme tasks of the movement to make this the dominant principle not only for its own ranks, but for the entire state as well.*

*He who would be a leader shall have the highest, unlimited authority; he also shall bear the final and heaviest responsibility.*

*He who is not capable of that, or is too cowardly to bear the consequences of his actions, is not fit to be a leader. Only the hero is called. . . .*

Adolf Hitler, *Mein Kampf* (Munich, 1939), pp. 378–79.

. . . *Starting with our profound understanding of this point, let us fashion the principles and tendencies of a movement which, in our opinion, are the only ones that could not merely halt the decline of the German people, but could create the granite foundation of a future state which will not be an un-German mechanism of economic groups and interests, but a folkish organism:* A Teutonic State of The German Nation.

Hitler, *Mein Kampf*, pp. 361–62.

## THE STRUGGLE BETWEEN LIGHT AND DARK: THE IDEOLOGY

Hitler also very much retained the party's anti-Semitism. What he did with it, however, was to place it at the core of his whole ideology, of his world view. That world view consisted of his vision of Social Darwinism.

Of all the components of the Nazi ideology—and under Hitler's guidance, a program was changing into an ideology, just as a party was changing into a movement—his pseudo-Darwinism was the one truly essential and entirely unalterable part. The *Führerprinzip* was important, but it was largely a means to an end, which was to control a state whose task it would be to sponsor a better race. The anticommunism was a constant element, but it, too, derived from Hitler's interpretation of natural selection; "the Jewish teaching of Marxism," he noted with disapproval in *Mein Kampf*, "rejects the aristocratic principle of nature, and replaces the eternal right of force and strength with the mass of numbers and deadweight." The intense nationalism was always present, but it was racial, not historical in kind; "never has a state been founded on a peaceful economy; it has been founded, always and solely, by the instinct for preserving the species." Like everything else in his philosophy, it, too, ultimately derived from his biological views.

Life, Hitler thought, was a perpetual struggle. It was a struggle between individuals. It was a struggle between races. And in its final essence, it was a struggle between good blood and bad, between the Nordic culture-creators and the Semitic culture-destroyers. Darwin was blending with H. S. Chamberlain, Haeckel with Wagner.

The first selection that follows is from an early Hitler speech; the second from *Mein Kampf*; the next from the "Eighty Maxims" of another Nazi leader, R. Walther Darré (1895–1953), the party's expert on agriculture; and the final one is from *Mein Kampf* again:

> . . . *It has ever been the right of the stronger, before God and man, to see his will prevail. History proves that he who lacks strength is not served in the slightest by "pure law." . . . All of nature is one great struggle between strength and weakness, an eternal victory of the strong over the weak. If it were any different, nature would be in a state of*

putrefaction. The nation which would violate this elementary law would rot away. . . .

Speech by Hitler on April 13, 1923, in Günter Schönbrunn, ed., *Weltkriege und Revolutionen* (Munich, 1961), p. 285.

. . . Everything that we admire today on this earth, science and art, technology and inventions, is the creative product of but a few nations and perhaps originally of but one race. It is on them that the existence of all culture depends. Should they perish, the beauty of this earth will perish with them.

. . . All great cultures of the past were destroyed only because the originally creative race died from blood poisoning.

The final cause of such decline was always the failure to remember that all culture is created by men, and not vice versa, so that if a certain culture is to be saved, the men creating it must be saved. Their preservation, however, is tied to the iron law of necessity, and to the right to victory on the part of the best and the stronger.

Therefore, he who would live, let him fight, and he who would not fight in this world of struggle is not deserving of life. . . .

Hitler, *Mein Kampf*, pp. 316–17.

To disregard the laws of our blood is to deny God's order in this world and to violate his command.

\*

Our nation's only true possession is its good blood.

\*

Germanic laws on marriage and eugenics can be understood only if they are seen for what they are: eugenic laws.

\*

All eugenic progress can begin only by eliminating the inferior, and by insisting on proven blood.

\*

By introducing eugenic considerations into our ideas of marriage, we do not introduce something that is more suitable to animals, or unworthy of man; no, in so doing we merely resume the best moral and intellectual traditions of our ancestors.

\*

Where the laws concerning the land were sound, and where marriage laws were sound, war has never yet been harmful, in a biological sense, to the Nordic race.

*

That is moral which supports the purity of the German race; that is immoral which hinders it.

> R. Walther Darré, 80 *Merksätze und Leit-sprüche über Zucht und Sitte* (Goslar, n. d. [c. 1937]), n. p.

. . . If one were to divide mankind into three species: the culture-creators, the culture-bearers, and the culture-destroyers, only the Aryan would be likely to fit the first definition. It is to him that we must trace the foundations and the walls of all that human beings have created.

. . . The most powerful antipode to the Aryan is the Jew. . . . No, the Jew possesses no culture-creating ability whatever, since he does not, and never did, have that quality without which man cannot truly develop toward a higher order: idealism. Therefore, his intellect will never act as a constructive force.

. . . He is and remains the typical parasite, a sponger who, like a malign bacillus, spreads more and more as long as he will find some favorable feeding ground. And the consequences of his existence, too, resemble those of the parasite: where he appears, the host nation will sooner or later die. . . .

> Hitler, *Mein Kampf*, pp. 318, 329, 332, and 334.

## IDEOLOGY: A MATTER OF TACTICS?

So constantly is the racial theme reiterated in *Mein Kampf* that the reader may suspect a largely tactical motive behind it. That motive—the wisdom of concentrating on but a single opponent—seems suggested by Hitler himself, both in his later actions, and in this passage from *Mein Kampf*:

. . . The art of all truly great national leaders has at all times primarily consisted of this: not to divide the attention of a people, but to concentrate that attention on a single enemy. The more unified the fighting spirit of a nation, the greater the magnetic attraction of a movement, the more forceful the power of its thrust. It is part of the genius of a great leader to make it appear as though even the most distant enemies belonged in the same category; for weak and fickle characters, if faced by many different enemies, will easily begin to have doubts about the justness of their cause.

As soon as the vacillating masses see themselves in a battle against too many enemies, they will immediately succumb to an objective view, and ask whether it can really be true that everybody else is wrong, and that only their own people or their own movement are right.

But if that happens, the first paralysis of your own strength sets in. Therefore, a great number of basically different enemies must always be described as belonging to the same group, so that as far as the mass of your followers is concerned, the battle is being waged against a single enemy. This strengthens the belief in the rightness of your cause, and increases the bitterness against those who would attack it. . . .

Hitler, *Mein Kampf*, p. 129.


## IDEOLOGY: A MATTER OF CONVICTION AND OF MENDELING THROUGH

But while Hitler, particularly in his foreign policy, came to master the art he so well described here—attributing all villainy to but one enemy at a time, and letting others wait their turn—his hatred of the Jews, and with it his whole pseudo-Darwinian philosophy, were very much more than a matter of political expediency. What was involved here were his most profound convictions. This was the way he felt; this was the rock-solid part of an ideology he had acquired in the Vienna of his youth and would never abandon.

The two documents that follow date from a much later period in his life, when he was at the height of his power. They were written in 1942, by an aide who had been instructed to take notes on Hitler's conversations in "the Chief's" headquarters.

. . . When Captain Bauer remarked that the number of passengers that could be carried in a commercial airplane would have to be increased from 60 to 100, the Chief said that there was no need to worry about that. The next decades would bring us passenger planes of a size to include a bathroom.

Even so, suggested Admiral Krancke, even with this extraordinary development of aviation, the passenger fleet need not fear the competition of the airplane. For he doubted that planes could be built that would be large enough to take the freight business in coal and lumber and iron away from ships. After all, the railways had left the transport of bricks to freighters.

The Chief ended the discussion by saying that one should take a developmental view of these things. Just as the bird represented a higher stage of development over the flying fish, and the flying fish a higher stage over the ordinary fish, so the ship was an early stage of the plane. But it was to the plane that the future belonged.

> (July 3, 1942) Henry Picker, *Hitlers Tischgespräche im Führerhauptquartier* (Second edition, Stuttgart, 1963), p. 431.

. . . After lunch, the Chief told about a certain Baron von Liebig. The baron was supposed to be very patriotic, and had therefore been introduced to him, too. He had been repelled, however, by the man's decidedly Jewish looks. But people had assured him time and again that according to the baron's genealogy, which reached back unusually far, there were no indications whatever of any admixture of Jewish blood. Now it accidentally turned out that some great-grand-ancestor of the baron, born in 1616 at Frankfurt, was the daughter of fully Jewish parents.

Thus 300 years lay between the Jewess and the present Baron von Liebig. And though this Jewess aside, there were none but Aryans among his ancestors, his appearance clearly showed the racial characteristics of the Jew. This confirmed what he [Hitler] had said about the Englishman, [Sir Stafford] Cripps, which was that in the case of mixed breeds—no matter how slight the Jewish share of the blood—in the course of the generations a pure Jew would always come Mendeling through. The Jewish race was tougher, that was it. . . .

> (July 1, 1942) Picker, *Hitlers Tischgespräche*, pp. 424–25.

## SUBPEOPLE

And it was the race issue that supplied the basic dogma for the most dedicated of Nazi groups. In 1942, the education division of the SS, the Nazi elite guard, issued a pamphlet entitled *Der Untermensch*—*Sub-Man*. In it, photographs of strong and noble Nordic types alternated with those of Slavs and Jews who displayed neither of these qualities. The introduction to the pamphlet read as follows:

## Sub-Man

As night rises against day, as light and shade are each other's eternal enemies, so the greatest enemy of man—of man, the master of this universe—is man himself.

Sub-man, the biologically apparently quite similar creation of nature, with hands, feet, and a sort of brain. But it is a very different sort of creature, a terrifying creature—a mere projection of a man. His features may resemble man, but intellectually, spiritually, he is lower than any animal. His inmost being is a cruel chaos of wild, unbridled passions— an unbounded will to destruction, the most primitive desires, undisguised baseness.

Sub-man, nothing else!

For not all is equal that bears the human face.

Woe to him who forgets that!

Whatever this earth has produced by way of great works, thoughts, and arts, man has thought of it, created it, completed it. Man contemplated, man invented. Man had but one aim: to work his way up to a higher existence, to complete the incomplete, to replace the imperfect with the better.

Thus culture grew.

Thus the plow came into existence, thus tools, thus the house.

Thus man became social. Thus the family was created, and the nation, and the state. Thus man became good and great. Thus he excelled all other living creatures.

Thus he became God's neighbor!

But sub-man lived, too. He hated the work of the other. He raged against it—secretly, as a thief; publicly, as a slanderer, as a murderer. Like found like.

Beast called to beast.

Never did sub-man give peace. For what he needed was semidarkness, was chaos.

He shunned the light of cultural progress.

What he needed for his self-preservation was the morass, was hell, not the sun.

And this sub-world of sub-man found its leader: the eternal Jew! . . .

SS Hauptamt-Schulungsamt, *Der Untermensch* (Berlin, [1942]), n. p., in Himmler files ("Reichsführer SS und Chef der Deutschen Polizei, Persönlicher Stab, Schriftgutverwaltung") of Hoover Institution, Box 11. (See also the correspondence about the publication in the same file.)

## THE PUBLIC FACE: FREEDOM,
## BREAD, HONOR

This sort of open invitation to genocide came later, however. In the Twenties, the Nazis tended to stress matters on which a majority of Germans could agree: the greatness of the nation and the wickedness of Versailles, efficiency in government and the need for a prosperous economy. The slogan that appeared over the masthead of the *Völkische Beobachter*, the party's official newspaper, during the twenty-five years of its existence read not "Race and Blood," but "Freedom and Bread."

It was true, of course, that Hitler had made no secret of his actual views in *Mein Kampf*. But in the first place, the book was pretty well unreadable as a whole. It would probably be a fair estimate to say that the number of Nazis who owned but did not read a copy of *Mein Kampf* was roughly equal to the number of Communists with a similar approach toward *Das Kapital*. In the second place, some of those who did read it, and liked certain parts of it, or were impressed by Hitler as a speaker, could feel that the racial passages were so clearly absurd that the Nazis, if they were ever in power, would obviously have to abandon this part of their ideology.

The following selections give some indication of the public face of Nazism. The first is from *Mein Kampf*, and shows that Hitler, on occasion, was quite capable of presenting even his racial theories in more pleasing terms. The second is from the *Myth of the Twentieth Century*, by Alfred Rosenberg (1893–1943), editor of the *Völkische Beobachter*, and the party's official philosopher. It is a frank enough passage, and the totality of the claim that speaks from it is apparent today; but at the time, the restoration of the nation's honor did matter more than anything else to many Germans. The third and fourth selections are from Dr. Joseph Goebbels (1897–1945), the party's propaganda expert, and demonstrate even more clearly the Nazi strategy for wininng voters. (The "Common Interest Before Self-Interest" passage is from a pamphlet that first appeared in 1926 and was reprinted many times; the other is from a speech given in 1944 before a group of German generals.) The next selection, putting things even more briefly, and vaguely, is by Hermann Göring (1893–1946), World War I flying ace, and as close to being second in command to Hitler as anyone ever came in the Nazi movement. The final passage is from one of the autobiographies in the Abel file, recording an early Nazi's recollections of the Twenties, and what he, a miner from the Saarland, considered to be the slanders against the party.

> . . . What we must fight for is to safeguard the survival and growth of our race and nation; is to feed its children and to maintain the purity of the blood; is to secure the freedom and independence of our fatherland—so that our nation, too, might grow in maturity to fulfill the mission which the creator of the universe has assigned to it. . . .

Hitler, Mein Kampf, p. 234.

> . . . The idea of honor, of national honor, is the beginning and the end of all our thought and action. There can be no other center of strength of equal worth—not Christian charity, not Masonic humanity, not Roman philosophy. . . .

Alfred Rosenberg, Der Mythos des 20. Jahrhunderts (433<sup>rd</sup> thousand, Munich, 1935), p. 514.

## The Common Interest Before Self-Interest

What is the first commandment of every National Socialist?
Love Germany more than anything, and your fellow Germans more than yourself!
What is the aim of the National Socialist idea of liberty?
To create the national community of all honestly creative Germans!
What is the content of that national community?
Freedom and bread for every German!
Who is a fellow German, a racial comrade?
Every honestly creative German is, provided his blood, his customs, his culture are German, and provided he speaks the German tongue!
What is the basic economic principle with which National Socialism wishes to replace the present economic warfare of all against all?
The Common Interest Before Self-Interest!

## The True National Socialist

What does it mean to be a National Socialist?
To be a National Socialist means nothing but: Fight, Faith, Work, Sacrifice!
What do we National Socialists want for ourselves?
Nothing!

What do we National Socialists want for the creative German
people?
Freedom!
What ties us National Socialists together, in this fight for Germany's
freedom, within and without our borders?
The awareness of belonging to a community of fate, a community
imbued with a spirit of radical innovation, a community whose mem-
bers shall be companions, one to the other, in good times and in bad.
What is the National Socialist password to freedom:
God helps those who help themselves!!!

> Joseph Goebbels, *Das kleine abc des Na-
> tionalsozialisten* (Elberfeld: n. d.), pp. 3
> and 22.

. . . Fifty or a hundred years from now, National Socialism, too,
will have become a philosophic system that can be studied at the
universities for four or five semesters, just as today, theology or classical
economics are academic subjects. If at such a time, I should ask a representative of National Socialism, "Can you tell me in a word what you
mean by National Socialism?" he would give me the same answer to the
question which I now will. It is this. The difference between National
Socialism and all previous systems, particularly the system it is now conquering, is that its starting point is the community, not the individual.
This gives a very different character to all our social ideas. What I
mean when I say war, or society, or economics, or political philosophy,
all these things suddenly appear from a different angle. We do not see
these things from the point of view of the individual, but from that of
the community. The basic principle with which we brought the whole
German people to follow us was a very simple one. It was "The Common Interest Before Self-Interest." . . .

> Joseph Goebbels, *Der Krieg als Weltan-
> schauungskampf* (Berlin, c. 1944), p. 9.

. . . How often have people asked me: "Come now, what is your
program?" Proudly, I could point to our simple and good storm troopers
and say: "There stand the bearers of our program. It is inscribed on
their free and open faces, and the program reads 'Germany!' " . . .

> Hermann Göring, *Aufbau einer Nation*
> (Berlin, 1934), p. 36.

. . . *People reproached me with accusations that the Hitler movement was the destroyer of both Christian churches, that it would remove all crippled and useless people, that it would dissolve the unions
and thus threaten labor's rights, that social insurance would come to an
end, and that what the Nazis wanted was another war, and many other
such things. When I heard these lies and slanders, I tried to enlighten
people, and I enjoyed what I was doing more and more when I saw that
in our town, too, the Nazi movement was growing, and receiving an
ever increasing number of votes in each election. . . .*

> Autobiographical sketch (1934) of Johann
> Schnur, in the Abel file of the Hoover In-
> stitution.

## THE IDEOLOGY: HITLER

We are not told just how he did enlighten the slanderers. Nor was
rational argument one of Nazism's strong points. And the necessity
became a virtue. National Socialism—and this can make any logical
exposition of the component parts of its ideology quite misleading—in
the last analysis was a revolt against rational thought. For reason, it
substituted faith—faith in "the movement," faith, to an even greater
degree, in Hitler. "Our program, in two words, reads 'Adolf Hitler,'" a
Nazi leader wrote as early as 1924. It was a more accurate description
than Göring's one word program.

The first selection is from the "Breviary of a Young National Socialist," written by a 22-year-old law student and Hitler Youth leader. The
second is from the party's official appeal to the voters in the presidential
election of 1932.

. . . *Even the most profound, the most learned of intellects touches
the surface of things only. Everything of which we are conscious, all
that is thinkable and understandable, is but thin snow on the high
mountains of the unconscious, snow that will quickly melt under the
storms of fate, of some intoxication, of the trembling of the soul. Life
would rather hide its ultimate secrets in a small folksong heard in the
village night than in fat and scholarly books. It is vain to try to plumb
the depths. We will never, by ourselves, be able to learn the essential.
All we can do is be moved by it.*

> Gottfried Neesze, *Brevier eines jungen
> Nationalsozialisten* (Oldenburg, 1933),
> p. 21.

. . . The National Socialist movement, assembled, at this hour, as a fighting squad around its leader, today calls on the entire German people to join its ranks, and to pave a path that will bring Adolf Hitler to the head of the nation, and thus

# Lead Germany to Freedom.

**Hitler** is the password of all who believe in Germany's resurrection.

**Hitler** is the last hope of those who were deprived of everything: of farm and home, of savings, employment, survival; and who have but one possession left: their faith in a just Germany which will once again grant to its citizens honor, freedom, and bread.

**Hitler** is the word of deliverance for millions, for they are in despair, and see only in this name a path to new life and creativity.

**Hitler** was bequeathed the legacy of the two million dead comrades of the World War, who died not for the present system of the gradual destruction of our nation, but for Germany's future.

**Hitler** is the man of the people hated by the enemy because he understands the people and fights for the people.

**Hitler** is the furious will of Germany's youth, which, in the midst of a tired generation, is fighting for new forms, and neither can nor will abandon its faith in a better German future. Hence Hitler is the password and the flaming signal of all who wish for a German future.

All of them, on March 13, will call out to the men of the old system who promised them freedom and dignity, and delivered stones and words instead: We have known enough of you. Now you are to know us!

# Hitler Will Win, Because
# The People Want His Victory!

**Munich, March 1, 1932**

## The National Leadership of the National Socialist German Workers' Party

*Völkischer Beobachter* (Bavarian edition), March 3, 1932, p. 1.

## THE IDEOLOGY'S APPEAL:
## WHY HERMANN FÜHRBACH JOINED

The election appeal did not quite work. Hindenburg, not Hitler, still was the winner in 1932. But Hitler had received 13 million votes. Nazi strength was increasing. The times were right. The war's memories might be fading, but the depression was very much present. "Unemployment meant hopelessness," Wilhelm Kaisen, Social Democrat and for many years Lord Mayor of Bremen recalled after 1945. "When we Germans cannot work, we go crazy."

The statistical tables show the relationship between economic misery in Germany (as expressed here in unemployment figures) and the votes received by Germany's six largest parties between 1924, when the Nazis first appeared on a national ballot, and 1932, the last free election before Hitler's accession to power. The employment figures, it is worth noting, tell only a part of the story. It was not merely that the unemployed who were not registered with the labor offices were not listed, but the number of unemployed union members—45 per cent in 1932—was disproportionately high. In other words, the true figures were worse than here indicated, and among the employed, there was a major shift from the 40-hour week, and skilled, well-paid labor, to badly paid, less skilled, and part-time labor. (The total population, by the way, was roughly half that of the United States in the same period, rising from 62 million in 1924 to 66 million in 1932.)

The autobiographical sketch that follows the tables describes how a variety of conditions and impressions—the lost war and the occupation, the pleasures not only of believing but of being able to do battle for these beliefs, whether one could define them or not—caused one man to join, and stay with, the Nazi party.

*I, Hermann Führbach, was born on December 9, 1907, in Mühl-heim-Glatz, the son of the building contractor Carl Führbach, and attended the Catholic primary school until I was fourteen. When the war broke out—I was seven years old—my eldest brother Carl received his call to join the 135th Infantry Regiment; my brother Wilhelm, even though he had not yet finished his apprenticeship, volunteered for the navy. Their patriotic enthusiasm had its effects on me too. Thus, even as a boy, I carried the guns of departing soldiers to the railway station for them. Every time that the army communiqué reported a new German victory, I enthusiastically ran to the church and helped ring*

ELECTIONS TO THE GERMAN REICHSTAG, 1924–1932

| | May 4, 1924 | December 7, 1924 | May 20, 1928 | September 14, 1930 | July 31, 1932 | November 6, 1932 |
|---|---|---|---|---|---|---|
| Number of Eligible Voters (in millions) | 38.4 | 39.0 | 41.2 | 43.0 | 44.2 | 44.2 |
| Votes Cast (in millions) | 29.7 | 30.7 | 31.2 | 35.2 | 37.2 | 35.7 |
| National Socialist German Workers Party | 1,918,000 6.6% | 908,000 3% | 810,000 2.6% | 6,407,000 18.3% | 13,779,000 37.3% | 11,737,000 33.1% |
| German Nationalist People's Party (Conservative) | 5,696,000 19.5% | 6,209,000 20.5% | 4,382,000 14.2% | 2,458,000 7% | 2,187,000 5.9% | 3,131,000 8.8% |
| Center Party (Catholic) | 3,914,000 13.4% | 4,121,000 13.6% | 3,712,000 12.1% | 4,127,000 11.8% | 4,589,000 12.4% | 4,230,000 11.9% |
| Democratic Party (The German State Party) | 1,655,000 5.7% | 1,921,000 6.3% | 1,506,000 4.9% | 1,322,000 3.8% | 373,000 1% | 339,000 1% |
| Social Democratic Party | 6,009,000 20.5% | 7,886,000 26% | 9,153,000 29.8% | 8,576,000 24.5% | 7,960,000 21.6% | 7,251,000 20.4% |
| Communist Party | 3,693,000 12.6% | 2,712,000 9% | 3,265,000 10.6% | 4,590,000 13.1% | 5,370,000 14.3% | 5,980,000 16.9% |

UNEMPLOYMENT IN GERMANY, 1924–1932[1]

| 1924 | 1928 | 1930 | July 31, 1932 | October 31, 1932 |
|---|---|---|---|---|
| 978,000 | 1,368,000 | 3,076,000 | 5,392,000 | 5,109,000 |

[1] The figures are those of annual average unemployment, except for 1932, where some precise end-of-the-month figures are available, and the two dates that coincide with the Reichstag elections are given. The election statistics are from Harry Pross, Die Zerstörung der deutschen Politik (Frankfurt, 1959), p. 352; those on unemployment from Saitzow, Die Arbeitslosigkeit, pp. 148–49, and Statisches Jahrbuch, 1933, p. 19.*

the victory bells. When my brothers came back from the front on leave, and told their stories, I was thrilled. I was very strongly moved by the news that my eldest brother, shortly before the end of the war, was killed in Flanders; even before that, two cousins, second lieutenants both, had given their lives for the fatherland. The end of the war, and the revolution, are events which I can still remember vividly. What I felt to be a particular disgrace was an incident in which Red revolutionaries stopped some officers, and right in front of our eyes in the school yard ripped off their epaulets.

After finishing school, I was apprenticed to the Thyssen Company as a die worker. On my very first day there, I got to know the class struggle, as taught by Marxism: people tore the black, white, and red rosette[2] off my windbreaker and tried to force me to join a syndicalist union. Since I knew no other way out, I applied for an apprentice membership in the German Metal Workers' Union.

It was in 1923 that I first heard about the Hitler movement. I quit the Metal Workers' Union and joined the defense league "German Eagle." Now everybody at the plant hated me. During every wildcat strike, I, as a German-minded boy, got my lumps from all sides. But I did not allow myself to be deterred from my path. When the French marched in, during the so-called Ruhr Invasion,[3] I got a lot of work from the defense league "German Eagle." Whenever possible, we got the facts on French troop strength and precise information on their equipment—guns, trucks, etc. At the end of 1925, we took a night march to Kettwig, from which we did not return until seven the next morning, because of the detours we were forced to make on account of the French. It was on the day the French departed from Mülheim, on that day of all days, that I was fired from my apprentice's job for my folkish convictions. On the evening of that same day, we showed the black, white, and red flag, and performed the stage play Tauroggen.[4] Marxists and Communists on this occasion wanted to tear the uniforms off us. For two weeks, we showed the play, and for two weeks we had to guard our uniforms, which after all we needed for our performance, day and night.

From this time on, the number of our adherents grew. At the end of 1925, Dr. Goebbels founded the local group Mülheim-Ruhr of the

[2] The colors were those of the old empire; the new republic's colors were black, red, and gold.

[3] In January 1923, the French, charging that the Germans had fallen behind on their reparations payments, moved units of their army into the Ruhr Valley, Germany's industrial heartland. Two years later, faced by German resistance and British diplomatic disapproval, the French withdrew again.

[4] It was at Tauroggen, in the winter of 1812, that General Yorck, commander of the Prussian corps serving with Napoleon, made an agreement with the Russians to withdraw from the fighting. It was a private agreement, but it cleared the way for Russia's declaration of war against France the following year.

National Socialist German Workers' Party, which I joined immediately. From that point on, I fought untiringly against Communists,
Marxists, Center party people, and fellow travelers. On July 4, 1926,
at the second National Socialist Party Congress, I took the oath on
the flag before the Führer, the first man from Mülheim to do so, a
member of storm troop detachment No. 26. It was only now that I
knew that Germany had a leader again. Our work never ended, even
if it was only a matter of providing protection for meetings, or dis-
tributing leaflets, or other such things. We were persecuted day and
night. We were called day-dreamers, and the Center party people
insulted us with names like Nazi kids and pagans.

September 1930 was the most difficult of the election battles for us.
We kept going day and night. During the day, we distributed leaflets;
at night, we stuck up our posters; in the evening, we were ordered to
duty at meetings. If we slept much, it was for two hours, on the bare
floor of the Lion Inn. On the evening of September 14, our reward
came—our great victory! Our slogan, "Awaken, Germany!" had had
its effect. One hundred seven National Socialist deputies were elected
to the Reichstag. Enthusiasm was great. The Jews were packing their
bags, many were already running away, but they came back a short
time later.

So we had to fight on, without flinching. But people were beginning to be afraid of us. The party organization was banned, and we
had to take off our brown shirts. If we put on white ones instead, as
we turned up to protect a meeting, the police beat us out of the hall
with rubber truncheons. If we all wore blue caps, or black ties, we
were subversive elements too. The Communists bludgeoned us down,
the police put us in prison, comrades were shot in the back. None
of this could stop us; it could only strengthen us in our resolve to
bring about the breakthrough of Adolf Hitler's idea among the German people. We were firm in our faith that one fine day we would
have won our battle for the unity of the German people. We pushed
ever deeper into the ranks of the Communists and the Marxists, and
brought the best of them over to us. The Center party people fought
us with particular bitterness; Catholic priests refused church funerals to
dead comrades. We were not allowed to enter church in uniform, even
though, as National Socialists, our basis is a Christian one.

Yet in spite of all hostility, we advanced slowly but all the more
surely. On January 30, 1933, Adolf Hitler created a united German
people. The great point of his program, to give work again to 8 million
unemployed, is being fulfilled more quickly than expected. Just in this
first year alone, millions went back to work. I, too, am to be counted
among those fortunate people. Untiringly now, we are working, and
helping to construct the National Socialist state, until every German
will understand the National Socialist ideology, faithful to our oath:

*For our leader and his idea we shall fight unto death.*

s. FÜHRBACH

Hermann Führbach
Mülheim-Ruhr
Gerber St. 1

Abel file, Hoover Institution at Stanford.

# 4

## POWER

President Hindenburg thanks you, Herr Hitler, for being willing to head a Presidential Cabinet. But he believes that he cannot reconcile it with his responsibilities before the German people to give his Presidential authority to the leader of a party which time and again has emphasized its exclusiveness. . . . Under these circumstances, the President must fear that a Presidential Cabinet headed by you must necessarily evolve into a party dictatorship. . . .

State Secretary Meissner to Adolf Hitler, November 24, 1932.

Mein Führer! Thus, on this day, I step before your picture, This picture is superdimensional and nearly limitless; it is powerful, hard, beautiful, and sublime; it is so simple, kind, modest, and warm; yea, it is father, mother, and brother in one, and it is more. It carries within it the greatest years of my life; it embraces the quiet hours of reflection, the days full of worries and fears, the sun of faith and fulfillment, the victory which is forever the beginning of new duties and new fields. The more I attempt to comprehend it, the larger, brighter, and more endless it becomes, yet without once feeling strange or distant.

Das Schwarze Korps, weekly of the SS, on Hitler's birthday, April 20, 1939.

## THE PRESIDENT'S OATH

Ever since the Nazis had emerged in 1932, as Germany's strongest single party, it was a matter not of whether but of when they would have to be entrusted with some share in the government. Only two major factors delayed their assumption of office. One was Hitler's insistence on leading the government; he would settle for nothing less than the chancellorship. The other was President von Hindenburg's instinctive distrust of Hitler; Hindenburg, the monarchist at heart, was becoming one of the Weimar Republic's last defenders. The following is taken from the minutes of a conversation between Hindenburg and Hitler held on August 13, 1932. (A second conversation between them, held three months later, was to result in the same impasse.)

> President von Hindenburg opened the conversation by telling Herr Hitler that he was prepared to let the National Socialist Party and its leader Hitler participate in the government of the Reich, and that he would welcome their cooperation. He then asked Herr Hitler whether he was prepared to join the present von Papen government. Herr Hitler declared that for reasons which he had explained to Chancellor von Papen at some length that morning, joining the present gevernment, or cooperating with it, was out of the question. Considering the importance of the National Socialist movement, he would have to demand the full and complete leadership of government and state for himself and his party.
> President von Hindenburg thereupon stated emphatically that he had to respond to this demand with a clear and determined "No." He could not, before God, his conscience, and the fatherland, bear the responsibility of entrusting all governmental authority to a single party, a party moreover, which held to such a one-sided attitude toward people with convictions different from theirs. . . .

Memorandum by State Secretary Meissner, in Walther Hubatsch, *Hindenburg und der Staat* (Göttingen, 1966), p. 338.

## IN POWER: A CALL TO ALL

But Hindenburg was old, and the Nazis, while declining slightly in voter appeal toward the end of 1932, still outpolled every other single party by a wide margin. On January 30, 1933, the President gave in, and agreed to appoint Hitler Chancellor. The cabinet over which Hitler was to preside contained only two other Nazis, however. The remaining eight ministers were either Conservatives or nonpolitical experts. They would, so the calculation of the President's advisers went, lead the Nazis in their midst to civilized habits. It was a miscalculation. What really had happened on January 30, was Hitler's triumph, was, as a (Viennese) observer put it, that "the Prussian sword had been placed in the hands of Austrian foolishness." But the new government's first proclamation, on February 1, 1933, still breathed the spirit of Conservative respectability. It was a public façade that Hitler did not yet find it useful to discard.

> . . . Thus the new national government will consider it its first and supreme duty to restore our nation's unity of will and spirit. It will safeguard and defend the foundations on which the strength of our nation rests. It will firmly protect Christianity, the basis of our entire morality; it will safeguard the family, the nucleus of our body politic and our state. It will, beyond estates and classes, make our people aware again of its national and political unity, and the duties that evolve therefrom. It wants to base the education of Germany's youth on a reverence for our great past, on pride in our old traditions. It will thus declare war on spiritual, political, and cultural nihilism. Germany must not and will not become prey to anarchic Communism.
>
> In place of turbulent instincts, the government will once again make national discipline our guide. In so doing, it will consider with great care all institutions which are the true guarantors of the strength and power of our nation.
>
> The national government will solve the great task of reorganizing our nation's economy in two great Four Year Plans:
>
> Saving the German farmer, so that the nation's food supply and thus the very basis of its existence shall be secured.
>
> Saving the German worker by a powerful and comprehensive attack on unemployment. . . .

> Appeal of the government to the German people, February 1, 1933, in Johannes Hohlfeld, ed., *Dokumente der Deutschen Politik und Geschichte* (Berlin, n. d.), IV, 8–9.

## CHANCELLORSHIP INTO DICTATORSHIP: THE CONTROL OF POLITICAL LIFE

It was not a façade Hitler cared to maintain for very long, however. With great speed and skill, he proceeded to transform the legal, limited powers of his office into the equally legal but total control of the state. Using the governmental instability of Weimar as one excuse, and the specter of a Communist threat as another, even more effective one (the Reichstag fire, in February 1933, whose origins are unclear to this day, was particularly useful in that connection), he either took over or destroyed all institutions that might interfere with his intention to direct German life in its totality. Opposition newspapers were taken over or banned. The unions were dissolved, and replaced with a Nazi "Labor Front." All political parties, save his own, were outlawed one by one. A bill was passed that enabled Hitler to govern without parliament. And when Hindenburg died, in 1934, Hitler made himself head of state as well as head of government, and received an overwhelming popular vote of approval for thus combining the offices of Chancellor and President.

Effective opposition to all these measures was kept to a minimum by two principal means. One was repression and intimidation. The first concentration camps came into existence early in 1933, as did a well functioning political police apparatus. The other was propaganda and conversion. In the spring of 1933, Dr. Goebbels entered the government to fill the newly created post of Minister of Public Enlightenment and Propaganda, took control of all public communications media, and used them superbly.

The three documents that follow indicate the major legal steps that converted Hitler's chancellorship into his dictatorship.

## Law for Terminating the Suffering of People and Nation of March 24, 1933

The Reichstag has passed the following law,[1] which has been approved by the Reichsrat.[2] The requirements of legal Constitutional change having been met, it is being proclaimed herewith.

### Article 1

In addition to the procedure outlined for the passage of legislation in the Constitution, the government[3] also is authorized to pass laws. This applies equally to legislation specified in Articles 85, paragraph 2, and 87 of the Constitution.[4]

---

[1] The law received well over the two-thirds majority required by the Weimar Constitution for such extraordinary legislation. The Communist party was already outlawed, and its deputies were unable to cast their votes. The other parties were induced to vote for it by a mixture of threats and promises. Only the Social Democrats voted against it.

[2] The upper house, made up of the representatives of the German federal states.

[3] The German term is *Reichsregierung*, i.e. the administrative branch of the government, or the cabinet.

[4] These dealt with parliament's special authority over taxation.

## ARTICLE 2

Laws passed by the government may deviate from the Constitution, provided they do not deal with the institutions, as such, of Reichstag and Reichsrat. The prerogatives of the President continue unchanged.

## ARTICLE 3

The laws passed by the government shall be issued by the Chancellor and published in the official gazette. In the absence of contrary provisions, they shall enter into effect on the day after they have been published. Articles 68 to 77 of the Constitution[5] do not apply to laws passed by the government.

## ARTICLE 4

Treaties with foreign nations which bear on matters of domestic law do not require the approval of the institutions involved in such domestic legislation. The government shall decide on the regulations necessary to implement such treaties.

## ARTICLE 5

The law is valid as of the day it is proclaimed. Its terminal date is April 1, 1937; it shall also cease to be in force if the present government should be replaced by another.

Berlin, March 24, 1933

> The President
> s. VON HINDENBURG
> The Chancellor
> s. ADOLF HITLER
> The Minister of the Interior
> s. FRICK
> The Minister of Foreign Affairs
> s. BARON VON NEURATH
> The Minister of Finance
> s. v. KROSIGK

> Hans-Adolf Jacobsen and Werner Jochmann, eds., *Ausgewählte Dokumente zur Geschichte des Nationalsozialismus 1933–1945* (Bielefeld, 1961), I, n. p.

[5] These dealt with the procedures to be observed for enacting new legislation.

## Law Against the New Formation of Parties of July 14, 1933

The government has passed the following law, which is being proclaimed herewith:

### ARTICLE 1

The sole political party existing in Germany is the National Socialist German Workers' Party.

### ARTICLE 2

Whoever shall undertake to maintain the organization of another party, or to found a new party, shall be punished with a sentence of hard labor of up to three years, or of prison between six months and three years, unless other regulations provide for heavier punishment.

Berlin, July 14, 1933

The Chancellor
s. ADOLF HITLER
The Minister of the Interior
s. FRICK
The Minister of Justice
s. GÜRTNER

Hohlfeld, *Dokumente*, IV, 83.

## Law Concerning the Head of the German State of August 1, 1934

The government has passed the following law, which is being proclaimed herewith:

### ARTICLE 1

The office of President shall be combined with that of Chancellor. Thus all the functions heretofore exercised by the President are transferred to the Führer and Chancellor Adolf Hitler. He has the right to appoint his deputy.

ARTICLE 2

*This law is in force as of the date of the death of President von Hindenburg.*

Hohlfeld, *Dokumente*, IV, 175.


# CHANCELLORSHIP INTO DICTATORSHIP:
## THE ALIGNMENT OF NONPOLITICAL
## ORGANIZATIONS


The control of Germany's political institutions was but one part of the story. Another was the control of all kinds of cultural and professional organizations. It was the totality of German life that the Nazis meant to refashion. From chess clubs to medical associations, from lawyers' guilds to little theater groups, the policy was that of "Gleichschaltung"—of "alignment" with Nazi principles and Nazi practice. A very few members of these organizations resigned in protest, some went along grudgingly, and many cooperated enthusiastically. And it was the latter who were heard. (André Maurois's phrase about Napoleon's coup of Brumaire applies here too, "France had not been raped; she had yielded.")

The first selection is from a speech by Hitler at the 1933 Nuremberg party rally, in which he very frankly outlined the motives behind Gleichschaltung. The second comes from the annual report for 1933 of the German Mathematical Association. The third is from the introduction of a book on "Our Rabbits."


On January 30, 1933, the National Socialist Party was entrusted with the political leadership of the country. The end of March saw the outward conclusion of the National Socialist revolution—a conclusion insofar as taking complete possession of political power was concerned. But only a person who truly failed to comprehend the essence of this mighty struggle could believe that it meant the conclusion of the battle between ideologies. This would only have been the case had the National Socialist movement wanted nothing more than what the customary political parties did. These parties indeed are in the habit of reaching, on the day they assume power, the zenith of their desires and their existence. Ideologies, however, consider the assumption of *power nothing but a prerequisite for the fulfillment of their true mission. . . .*

Adolf Hitler, September 1, 1933; *Reichstagung in Nürnberg 1933* (Berlin, 1934), pp. 75–76.

. . . We wish thus to conform to the spirit of the total state, and to cooperate loyally and honestly. Unconditionally and joyfully, we place ourselves—as is a matter of course for every German—at the service of the National Socialist movement and behind its leader, our Chancellor Adolf Hitler. And we hope that we have something to offer. What mathematics and natural science mean in today's state, too, for patriotic education, will be indicated in the address by Senior Counselor [Oberstudiendirektor] Ernst Tiedge.

But we also know that even in a merely advisory capacity, we are in a position to be heard only if in external matters, too, we adapt ourselves to the demands of the movement.

Hence, we decided to submit these three points for your approval:

1. The leadership principle. You are to elect a leader, who is to bear the sole responsibility.

2. The leader then is to appoint his assistants, and especially the members of a leader's council. In so doing, he shall be obliged to observe the requirements of Aryan ancestry in their strictest form, i.e., as they apply to leading government officials.

3. The Association's board is to be dissolved. It is the prerogative of the leader to organize that institution in a new form. . . .

From the address of the President of the German Mathematical Association, September 20, 1933; *Jahresbericht der Deutschen Mathematiker-Vereinigung* (Leipzig, 1934), XLIII, 81–82.

. . . Since the National Socialist assumption of power, German rabbit breeding has made unheard of progress, German rabbit breeding received a new aim. The people concerned with it were imbued with new organizational and eugenic impulses. For the first time, a generally valid basis was given to breeding and keeping rabbits, which raised rabbit breeding from the unorganic state of former times to a major economic factor. . . .

José Filler, *Unsere Kaninchen* (Berlin, 1942) cited in Léon Poliakov and Josef Wulf, *Das Dritte Reich und seine Denker* (Berlin, 1959), p. 534.

## THE TOTAL STATE:
## "HITLER YOUTH"

The rabbits were an extreme example. Yet they indicated a trend (which selections on whaling under National Socialism or on Nordic bookbinding might have illustrated equally well). That trend was to follow the change from chancellorship to *Gleichschaltung* with that from "alignment" to the total state. The state ultimately wished to see no private sphere preserved. This applied, with particular force, to the education of youth. It was not only that the existing schools, from primary education on up, were Nazified, that undesirable teachers were removed, new ones hired, and the curriculum brought into line with Nazi ideology. The after-hours activities of children, from the age of six, were to be controlled as well, in a Nazi Youth organization which, as the following law will indicate, it was impossible to elude.

### *Law Concerning the Hitler Youth of December 1, 1936*

*It is on youth that the future of the German nation depends. Hence, it is necessary to prepare the entire German youth for its coming duties.*

*The government therefore has passed the following law, which is being proclaimed herewith:*

#### ARTICLE 1

*The entire German youth within the borders of the Reich is organized in the Hitler Youth.*

#### ARTICLE 2

*It is not only in home and school, but in the Hitler Youth as well that all of Germany's youth is to be educated, physically, mentally, and morally, in the spirit of National Socialism, to serve the nation and the racial community.*

#### ARTICLE 3

*The task of educating the entire German youth is entrusted to the Reich Youth Leader of the National Socialist German Workers'*

Party. *He thus becomes the "Youth Leader of the German Reich."*
*His office shall rank with that of a ministry. He shall reside in Berlin,*
*and be responsible directly to the Führer and Chancellor.*

*The administrative instructions and legal regulations necessary to*
*implement and supplement this law shall be issued by the Führer and*
*Chancellor.*
*Berlin, December 1, 1936.*

The Führer and Chancellor
s. ADOLF HITLER

Jacobsen and Jochmann, *Ausgewählte Do-*
*kumente,* I, n. p.

# THE TOTAL STATE:
# THE UNIVERSITIES

All phases of education, the universities included, were a matter of
Nazi concern. The two quotations that follow do not claim to give a
complete, or even a representative picture of German university life
under National Socialism. Not all professors were as politically naïve as
Martin Heidegger, or as obsessed with racial fantasies as Philipp Lenard.
Much excellent work, untainted by Nazi ideology, was carried on between 1933 and 1945, and a few professors even engaged in an active
resistance to the regime that was to cost them their lives. But the selections are representative of Nazi policy and Nazi intentions; this was the
direction that higher education was meant to take.

The first passage is from the speech given by one of existentialism's
great figures, Martin Heidegger (b. 1889), on the occasion of his becoming dean of the faculty at the University of Freiburg in May 1933. The
second is from the 1935 introduction to the four volume *German Physics*
by Philipp Lenard (1862–1947), professor of physics at Heidelberg, and
winner of the Nobel Prize for his discoveries on cathode rays.

. . . *The much praised "academic freedom" shall be driven out of*
*Germany's universities, for this freedom, being merely negative, was*
*not genuine. What it meant primarily was unconcern, was a capri-*
*cious exercise of intentions and inclinations, was noncommitment. The*

concept of a German student's freedom is now being returned to its true meaning. It is from this true meaning that the future bonds and obligations of the German student shall devolve.

The first bond is that with the national community. It imposes an obligation to take part, in thought and deed, in the endeavors, the desires, and the skills of all classes and all members of the nation. This bond shall henceforth be firmly established, and rooted in the student's existence, by the Labor Service.

The second bond is that with the honor and fate of the nation in the midst of other nations. It demands a readiness—secured by skill and education, and firmed by discipline—to put one's very life in the scales. This bond shall embrace and penetrate all student existence as Military Service.

The third student bond is that with the spiritual mission of the German people. This nation determines its fate whilst living its historical existence under the evident sign of the superiority of the political forces that shape the human condition, and whilst ever struggling anew for the attainment of its spiritual world. Thus exposed to the extreme precariousness of its own existence, this nation wishes to be a spiritual nation. It demands of itself, and for itself in its leaders and guardians, the hardest clarity of the highest, widest, richest knowledge. . . .

These three bonds—bonds that reach from the people to the fate of the nation in its spiritual mission—all emanate equally from the German soul. The three services to which they give life—Labor Service, Military Service, Knowledge Service—are equally essential and of equal rank. . . .

Martin Heidegger, *Die Selbstbehauptung der deutschen Universität. Rede, gehalten bei der feierlichen Übernahme des Rektorats der Universität Freiburg i. Br. am 27. 5. 1933* (Breslau, [1933]), pp. 15–17.

. . . "German physics?" people will ask. I might have said Aryan physics, too, or physics of Nordic man, physics of the truth-seekers and the reality-illuminators, physics of those who are the founders of natural science. "Science is and remains international!" people will want to object. But the objection proceeds from erroneous assumptions. In reality, science—like anything else created by man—is conditioned by blood and race. An illusion of internationality can be created by the fallacy of concluding that because the results of science are universally valid, its origins must be equally universal. Or else the illusion will be due to a failure to realize that people in other countries who pursued science in a manner identical or similar to that of the German people, could do so only because (and to the extent that) they, too, are or were of a predominantly Nordic racial mixture. People of different racial mixtures have different ways of pursuing science.

Of course, no nation so much as began research in the natural sciences unless it based it on the nourishing soil of the achievements already supplied by Aryans. The stranger at first joined in, and imitated, many things; it takes a fairly long development to reveal his peculiar racial characteristics. Considering the literature now available, it might already be possible to talk of a physics of the Japanese; in the past, there was a physics of the Arabs. A physics of the negroes is unknown; however, a peculiar physics of the Jews has been spreading far and wide. Until now, it has not been very much recognized as such, mainly because of the custom of categorizing a literature according to the language in which it is written. Jews are everywhere, and people who today still defend the international quality of science mean, probably quite unconsciously, Jewish science. That science, so much is true, can indeed be found wherever Jews are, and is the same everywhere.

It is important to take a brief look at the "physics" of the Jewish people, because it is the antithesis of German physics, and because it is only by contrasting the two that the nature of German physics will truly be illuminated for many. As with everything Jewish, it has only been recently that an unprejudiced inquiry into Jewish physics could take place. For a long time, Jewish physics had developed reluctantly and surreptitiously. With the end of the war, however, when the Jews came to dominate Germany and to set its fashions, it suddenly, and with all its racial peculiarities intact, burst forth like a flood. Soon, it also found zealous defenders among authors of non-Jewish, or at least not wholly Jewish blood. To characterize it briefly, it would be fairest and best to recall the activities of its probably most outstanding representative, the presumably pure-blooded Jew A. Einstein. His "relativity theories" were meant to reshape and dominate the whole science of physics, but when faced with reality, they lost all shred of validity.* Nor can one assume that they were ever intended to be true. The Jew is remarkably lacking in a feeling for truth, for a more than surface recognition of that reality which will exist no matter what men's thought processes might be. In this, he represents the opposite of the— concerned and boundless—will to truth of the Aryan researcher. . . .

Philipp Lenard, *Deutsche Physik in vier Bänden* (Second edition, Munich, 1938), I, ix–x.

* [Fn. in original:] It is a matter of course that the present work will nowhere need to deal with this mistaken intellectual structure. It will be seen that this will leave no gap in the connected and all-inclusive description of our total knowledge. The same applies to other "theories," unreal or uncertain, which are not mentioned. The fact that they will not be missed will be the best proof of their unimportance.

# THE LAW IN THE TOTAL STATE:
## THE THEORY

Aryan researchers in physics might be safely remote from everyday German life under National Socialism. Aryan law scholars were not. The three documents below indicate the principal Nazi theories on the law's functions. The first comes from a conference Hitler held with the Minister of Justice and his deputy, and sums up some long-held views. The second is by Carl Schmitt (b. 1888), author of several basic legal works, and for many years professor of law at the Universities of Berlin and Cologne. He is commenting on the so-called Röhm Purge of June 30, 1934, in which Hitler had several hundred people—many of them his former storm troop lieutenants—shot without a trial, for what he announced had been a plot against the state. (Actually, Hitler meant to draw the professionals of the regular army over to his side by eliminating Ernst Röhm, the chief of staff of the storm troopers, and an advocate of a broadly based people's army. He also used the occasion to settle a number of other and older political accounts.) The third selection, which dates from 1936, gives the guidelines issued by Hans Frank (1900–1946), leader of the German lawyers' guild under the Nazis, and President of the Academy for German Law.

. . . [HITLER:] *"Justice is no aim in itself. It serves to maintain man's social order, an organism to which we owe culture and progress. Each and every means which serves that purpose is right. Every means which no longer does is wrong. It is not the task of justice to be mild or tough. Its task simply is to serve that purpose.*

*". . . We must exterminate the idea that it is the judge's function to let the law prevail and if the world should perish. That is pure madness. It should be the other way around: the primary task is to secure the social order!"* . . .

Lothar Gruchmann, "Hitler über die Justiz,
Das Tischgespräch vom 20 August 1942,"
*Vierteljahreshefte für Zeitgeschichte,* XII,
98.

. . . *The Füher protects the law from its worst abuse if, in the moment of danger, he creates immediate justice on the authority of his leadership and thus of his supreme judgeship. "At this hour I was responsible for the fate of the German nation, and thus the supreme*

judge of the German nation." The true leader always is a judge as
well. Judgeship flows from leadership. He who would separate the two,
or even place them on opposite sides, makes the judge either into an
antileader, or into the tool of an antileader, and seeks to destroy the
state with the aid of the law. . . . In truth, the action of the Führer
was pure justice. It is not subject to the law; instead, it was the highest
law. . . .

> Carl Schmitt, *Positionen und Begriffe im*
> *Kampf mit Weimar-Genf-Versailles, 1923–*
> *1939* (Hamburg, 1940), p. 200.

1. The judge is not placed over the citizen as a government authority.
Instead, he stands in the ranks of the living community of the German
people. It is not his task to help apply a legal order that is higher than
the racial community, or to enforce some system of universal values.
What he must do, rather, is to safeguard the concrete order of the
racial community, to exterminate those who undermine it, to punish
behavior harmful to the community, and to arbitrate quarrels among
members of the community.

2. The basis for interpreting all legal sources is the National Socialist philosophy, especially as expressed in the party program, and
in the utterances of our Führer.

3. A judge has no right to examine a decision of the Führer which
has been issued in the form of a law or a decree. The judge is bound,
too, by other decisions of the Führer which clearly express a desire to
establish law.

4. Legal regulations issued prior to the National Socialist revolution
may not be applied if such application should violate today's healthy
emotions of the people. If a judge should suspend some legal regulation
with this in mind, it will be possible to obtain the decision of the
highest court on the matter.

5. To fulfill his task in the racial community, the judge must be
independent. He is not tied to instructions. The independence and
dignity of the judge make it essential to protect him properly against
efforts to influence him, and against unjustified attacks.

> Hans Frank, January 14, 1936; F. A. Six,
> ed., *Dokumente der deutschen Politik* (Ber-
> lin, 1942), IV, 337.

## THE LAW: THE PRACTICE

Practice, fortunately, did not in every case follow theory or even official guidelines. Some judges conformed outwardly, joined the obligatory

Nazi organizations and took care to adapt to Nazi terminology, but dispensed justice fairly and independently for as long as they could. (One clear limit to their influence, of course, was the institution of the concentration camps, in which any opponent of the regime could be held without recourse to judicial procedure.) Some passed slightly harsher sentences than they had before, but otherwise stayed within the spirit of accepted legal concepts. Others, however, did apply the new theories consistently and ruthlessly.

The purest institutional embodiment of National Socialist justice was the People's Court, established in 1934 to deal with crimes against the state. And its purest representative was Roland Freisler (1893–1945), the court's presiding judge, and author of the phrase, "Just is that which is useful to the German people."

The first passage below is an excerpt from the interrogation conducted by Judge Freisler in the session of the People's Court of August 7, 1944. The defendant is Major General Hellmuth Stieff, accused of complicity in the July 20 plot against Hitler's life. The passage is followed by a defense plea, delivered that same day, which is printed in its entirety.

. . . FREISLER: "All the same, now you knew the name of the man who was to pull the trigger. Did you report it to the Führer?"

STIEFF: "No."

FREISLER: "Is it a fact that a short time later, General Lindemann[6] turned to you with his defeatist worries?"

STIEFF: "He did talk to me several times, indicating his concern over the situation. I reject the term 'defeatist.' "

FREISLER: "You may reject the term 'defeatist.' That you may. What you reject interests me just as little as the perverted inclinations of some homosexual interest a healthy German man, for if you do not comprehend that this is the most outrageous defeatism, you are a political pervert. But it is our healthy opinion which matters here. Is it correct that you told Lindemann to talk to Olbricht?" [7]

STIEFF: "I did on that occasion say to him, 'Why don't you talk to Olbricht, too, about that.' "

FREISLER: "Why not talk to Olbricht about that! Well, we know now what role Olbricht played, and we'll be hearing some more details on it today. Did you talk to General Wagner[8] about the whole affair?

[6] General Fritz Lindemann, a codefendant of Stieff's.
[7] General Friedrich Olbricht, Deputy Commander of the Reserve Army, and long an opponent of Hitler.
[8] General Eduard Wagner, Quartermaster General of the German army, and another member of the anti-Hitler conspiracy.

STIEFF: *"Yes, I think it was in November or December of last year that I talked to him about it."*

FREISLER: *"Right, in the final months of the past year, 1943. Mr. Prosecutor General, I assume that we can extend the time span of the indictment to include 1943. (Agreement.) So he knew."*

STIEFF: *"General Wagner knew the whole situation. After all, I turned to him in the first place as to an older comrade."*

FREISLER: *"All I can say is Pfui Teufel! As to an older comrade? As to an older criminal, who as you know is aware of a plan to murder the Führer. A man you know to be aware of a plan to murder the Führer is no one's comrade; there is, as the old Germans used to say, open season on him as on a wolf. But if you want to talk about comradeship, he no longer was the older comrade, but the older criminal. Well then, you considered him the older criminal."*

STIEFF: *"No, I did not act from criminal motives."*

FREISLER: *"No. That is because in this area you are perverted, the way a homosexual is."*

STIEFF: *"No!"*

FREISLER: *"It is our opinion that is valid in this place, and no other opinion. What is valid here is the National Socialist view, and that is: with the Führer through thick and thin, to the last minute and beyond, and thus victory will be ours. Nothing else is valid. Everything else is defeatism, of which we want to hear nothing."*

STIEFF: *"Your Honor. In that case, I would have failed in my duty."*

FREISLER: *"Stop! Stop! If you are such a defeatist weak sister, you could have fulfilled your duty only by dying like the last Goths, who now live on within us. But I realize that your mind is dead to argument."* . . .[9]

Eugen Budde and Peter Lütsches, *Der 20. Juli* (Düsseldorf, 1952), pp. 41–42.

DEFENSE COUNSEL DR. L. SCHWARZ: *"As court-appointed defense counsel for the defendant Höppner [sic],[10] I examined, as is my official duty, the question of whether anything might be found in the facts ascertained in the pretrial investigation, in today's actual trial, or in the deposition of the defendant Höppner, that might be suitable for making a defense plea in favor of the defendant Höppner. After the speeches of the Prosecutor General and of my fellow defense counsel I need add nothing to characterize the deed of the defendant whom I have to represent. It would be an improper demand on the patience*

---

[9] General Stieff was sentenced to death the next day, August 8, as was General Lindemann. (As for the other two men mentioned in the interrogation, General Olbricht had been shot on July 20, and General Wagner had committed suicide three days later.)

[10] Major General Erich Hoepner, another codefendant of Stieff's.

of this court if I were to repeat, which I could, what was said on the matter by the gentlemen speaking before me. I also had to point out to the defendant Höppner, whom I have to represent, that as far as the degree of the penalty is concerned, it would hardly matter very decisively—in view of the crime with which he is charged—whether he was fully informed of the plans of his fellow conspirators or whether, up to a point, if I may use that expression, he perhaps, as it were, fell into the whole affair. He himself has been unable to deny that at a time, certainly, when active repentance might still have altered the course of events—a repentance that might have taken the form of reporting the intended crime, or at least of removing his own person from the group—he was aware of the full extent of what was being planned. He had known about it for weeks in advance, and he has so confessed to a degree that is at least legally sufficient.

"Under these circumstances, I find it impossible to take the floor for a defense plea in favor of the defendant Höppner. This defendant, too, knew what it meant to commit treason, to give aid and comfort to the enemy, and to subvert the armed forces. The law has provided the only possible punishment for that. As defense counsel, I have no submission to make to the People's Court." [11]

Budde and Lütsches, 20. Juli, p. 98.

## THE TOTAL STATE: ART

One more example may suffice to indicate the totality of the National Socialist claim. The example is that of the arts. Hitler, who as a youth had failed to pass the entrance examination to Vienna's school of architecture, had some pronounced ideas about the arts to which he held very firmly until the end of his life. What he favored was "sound," or "Nordic," art—particularly scenes of peasant life, and realistic nudes. What he regarded with disfavor was art alternately characterized as "Jewish," "cultural Bolshevik," or "degenerate." This in effect meant most modern, and particularly all abstract art, or, as he put it in *Mein Kampf*, "the sick excesses of mad or degenerate people, which have become familiar to us since the turn of the century under the collective terms of Cubism and Dadaism."

As Chancellor, he was in a position to do something about his tastes. All German painters and sculptors who wished to be able to work and exhibit were organized in a "National Chamber of Fine Arts." (There

[11] Sentence of death by hanging was passed on General Hoepner on August 8. It was executed the same day.

also were similar Chambers for writers, musicians, and actors, although the latter two, in particular, were not as a rule as tightly run as the Chamber of Arts.) Annual exhibits were held of officially approved German Art, in a vast museum specifically built for that purpose in Munich. These were accompanied by exhibits of "Degenerate Art," seized from various German museums or from the artists, and displayed under less than ideal conditions, with poor lighting, crowded walls, and mocking captions. What all this meant in one individual case is shown by the letter below. It is written by Professor Adolf Ziegler, President of the Chamber of Fine Arts (the academic title was bestowed by Hitler; Ziegler's specialty was detailed nudes) to one of Germany's leading expressionist painters and founding member of the group *Die Brücke.*

### THE PRESIDENT
#### OF THE NATIONAL CHAMBER OF FINE ARTS

*File Number*

*II B/ M756/870*

*Berlin W. 35*
*Blumenhof 4–6*
*Telephone 21 62 71*
*Postal Account No. 144430*

Registered!

*Mr. Karl Schmidt-Rottluff*
*Berlin W. 30*
*Bamberger St. 19*

*In connection with the task, entrusted to me by the Führer, of eradicating the works of degenerate art from our museums, no fewer than 608 paintings of yours had to be seized. A number of these paintings were displayed at the exhibits of Degenerate Art in Munich, Dortmund, and Berlin.*

*This fact could leave no doubt in your mind that your paintings did not contribute to the advancement of German culture in its responsibility toward people and nation.*

*Although you must also have been aware of the policy-setting speech of the Führer at the opening of the Great German Art Exhibit in Munich, the recent paintings of yours which you have now submitted to us indicate that even at this date, you are still far removed from the cultural foundations of the National Socialist state.*

*On the basis of these facts, I am unable to grant that you possess the necessary reliability for belonging to my Chamber. On the basis of Paragraph 10 of the first Executive Order implementing the Law Concerning the National Chambers of Culture of November 1, 1933 (Official Gazette, I, 797) I hereby expel you from the National Cham-*

ber of *Fine Arts* and forbid you, *effective immediately, any activity—professional or amateur—in the field of graphic arts.*

MEMBERSHIP BOOK No.
M 756

*issued in your name is no longer valid, and you are requested to send it back to me by return mail.*

s. ZIEGLER

Certified: DOEMLING
(*Rubber Stamp: National Chamber of Culture*
*Chamber of Fine Arts*)

Paul Ortwin Rave, *Kunstdiktatur im Dritten Reich* (Hamburg, 1949), p. 94.

## THE TOTAL STATE:
## THE MOTIVES

There were at least two common motives behind letters such as that to Schmidt-Rottluff, or scenes such as that provided by Freisler, or laws such as that which forced all Germans under 18 to join the Hitler Youth. One was that Hitler was in dead earnest about his various prejudices. Aryan, representational art was superior to experimental painting, no matter how indubitably Nordic a Schmidt-Rottluff's ancestry might be; the function of the law was to eradicate the state's enemies, real or potential; German youth was to be made more fit than any other youth. The other was that he had a shrewd idea that many people did not at all object to having their lives regimented. A passage from *Mein Kampf* describes that conviction with great frankness.

> . . . *The psyche of the great masses is not receptive to any half-measures or to any weakness.*
> *Like the female—whose soul, whose feelings, are shaped not so much by abstract reasoning as by an undefinable, emotional longing for a force that will complement hers, and who would therefore rather submit to the strong than dominate the weak—so a crowd loves a master better than a supplicant. In its inmost being, it will feel more fulfilled by a doctrine which will tolerate no others beside it than by the grant of liberal freedom. Nor does it, in most cases, really know what to do with the latter; rather, it will feel a bit deserted. The masses will not be conscious of the impudence with which they are being spiritually terrorized,*

*no more than they will be aware of the appalling mistreatment of
human liberty, for they have no feeling at all for the inner madness of
the whole doctrine. Thus all they will see are the ruthless force and the
brutality of the doctrine's clear-cut actions, and in the end, they will
always submit to these. . . .*

Hitler, *Mein Kampf,* p. 44.

## DER FÜHRERSTAAT: THE
## APOTHEOSIS OF HITLER

That the great majority did submit was beyond question. And the will
to which it submitted was not so much that of the state, in the traditional sense, or even that of the Nazi party; it was that of Hitler himself.
What mattered were Hitler's convictions and Hitler's desires. Germany
had become a *Führerstaat.* Germany was Hitler. Hitler was Germany.
And the Führer who was identical with the state could do no wrong and
think no wrong.

The first passage below was written by Göring in 1934. The second is
taken from a speech by Gauleiter Josef Bürckel (1895–1944), whom
Hitler had put in charge of the election campaign of January 1935 that
would return the Saarland (separated from Germany for fifteen years
by the Treaty of Versailles) to the Reich. The third comes from a collection of poems written by an unnamed group of Austrian Hitler
Youths, edited by Baldur von Schirach (b. 1907), head of the Hitler
Youth and "Youth Leader of the German Reich."

*. . . There is probably nobody else right now who attracts the gen-
eral interest as much as the Führer. And yet there is nobody whose
qualities are as difficult to describe as are those of Adolf Hitler. To
begin with, it does, of course, go without saying that for us who are his
followers—and anyone who knows the close relationship that exists
between Hitler and his men will understand that—there is no single
quality or characteristic of his which, to our eyes, he does not possess
to the highest perfection. If the Catholic Church is convinced that on
all matters of faith and morals, the Pope is infallible, then we National
Socialists declare, with the same inmost conviction, that for us, too, the
Führer is flatly infallible on all matters political as well as on all other
matters which affect the national and the social interests of the people.
What now is the secret of his powerful influence over his followers? Is
it his human kindness, his strength of character, or his unique modesty?
Is it perhaps his political talent of always correctly anticipating, and*

providing for, future events, or is it his outstanding courage or his special loyalty toward his men? I think that no matter what it is you look at, you will finally conclude that it is not the sum of all these virtues, but that there is something mystical, unsayable, almost incomprehensible about this man. And the person who does not intuitively sense that will never comprehend it, for we love Adolf Hitler, because we believe, with a faith that is deep and unshakable, that he was sent to us by God to save Germany. . . .

Göring, *Aufbau einer Nation*, pp. 51–52.

. . . Profoundly moving are the signs of German loyalty on the occasion of [the election of] January 13. A woman collapsed, dead, in a polling station. She had been allowed to confess her faith in her Germany; that happiness broke her heart. Another mother died of excitement even before reaching the voting booth. . . . Those, my Führer, are the people of the Saar. Their yearning is Germany! Their faith is Germany! Their loyalty is Germany! Adolf Hitler, be their protector! For you are Germany! Our Germany! . . .

Josef Bürckel, January 15, 1935; quoted in Schönbrunn, *Weltkriege*, p. 353.

## Profession of Faith in the Führer

Oft have we hearkened to your voice's sound
Listening quietly, folding our hands
While every word did penetrate our souls.
All of us know: the end must come
That will bring liberation from our needs.

What does a year mean when an age is changing!
What does a law mean that would hold us back.
What pulses through us, what provides direction
To our young lives is the pure faith you gave us.
You and none else, my Führer, are the way and end.

Baldur von Schirach, ed., *Das Lied der Getreuen* (Leipzig, 1941), p. 7.

# 5

## THE ATTRACTIONS

*That evil can appear in the shape of light, of good deeds, of historical necessity, of social justice, is plainly confusing to someone who comes from our traditional world of ethics. To the Christian, whose life rests on scripture, it is the confrontation with the unfathomable baseness of evil.*

Dietrich Bonhoeffer, "Ten Years After" (1942).

## A FEELING OF NATIONAL REBIRTH

If all that National Socialism had had to present to the German people had been paeans to the Führer, or racially pure mathematicians' associations, it would have been a very short-lived episode in modern German history. The fact of course was that it had to offer a great deal more. The crimes of the Nazi regime should not make us close our eyes to the achievements and attractions it offered at the time. There is small profit in seeing nothing but unrelieved evil in National Socialism, or in judging Hitler entirely from the vantage point of a generation endowed with hindsight.

To begin with, there was, in 1933, a feeling that things were moving again, that a new energy had been infused into German life. The first quotation comes from the memoirs of a Prussian nobleman, a man who, by upbringing and temperament, was anything but a true Nazi and who yet, with great succinctness and honesty, sums up what many people initially found attractive about the new regime. The other is taken from the diary of Erich Ebermayer, a popular playwright who had been trained as a lawyer, and whose father had been the German Attorney General.

. . . For a year and a half, from January 31, 1933, to the first large scale violation of all law, the Röhm purge, and to the unmasking of evil that followed it, Hitler (and with him National Socialism) for many of us was the savior from economic and social disaster, the unifier of the German people, the man who was restoring its honor abroad and raising it again to its proper rank among the European family of nations. . . .

> Arnold Freiherr von Vietinghoff-Riesch, *Letzter Herr auf Neschwitz* (Limburg, 1958), p. 204.

Frankfurt, March 28, 1933

. . . We are having lunch with the widow of my revered teacher, Privy Counsellor Freudenthal, professor of criminal law at Frankfurt University. A year ago, Freudenthal died, much too early. He had been a student of Liszt,[1] and one of the most modern of scholars in the field of criminal law. My father thought very highly of him, and Freudenthal was genuinely devoted to my father. His works on juvenile crime and on the punishment of juveniles are pioneering studies, which strongly influenced me and my own legal work, above all my doctoral dissertation. He and his clever, charming wife are Jewish.

The amazing thing about the meeting is that the young widow is not at all opposed to the Nazis. On the contrary, she lectures us on the outstanding qualities of Adolf Hitler, on the greatness of the age which we are allowed to witness, on the national rebirth, and is firmly convinced that no harm whatever will come to educated Jews in Germany.

I am hardly capable of comprehending this degree of delusion, turn to ice, and soon say my good-byes.

Nor does this seem to be an isolated case. Not long ago I was witness to a scene in Leipzig, in which the wife of Supreme Court Councillor Simonson, baptized and fully and obviously Jewish, told my father apropos of Hitler's latest Reichstag speech: "Isn't he like a Savior?" My stomach did a turn. . . .

> Erich Ebermayer, *Denn heute gehört uns Deutschland* . . . (Vienna, 1959), p. 49.

## A NEW COMMUNITY?

There was, along with the feeling of national rebirth, a new spirit of community. "Volksgemeinschaft"—the "national community"—was a

---

[1] Franz von Liszt (1851–1919), founder of the International Criminological Association.

term frequently used by the Nazis, and for a large number of people it had other and happier connotations than the racial one. The expectation was that Germany was finally developing into a more open, less class-conscious society. Some definite events and trends supported this. In the mid-thirties, for instance, the Nazis put so much pressure on the student fraternities, long the traditional strongholds of class privilege in Germany, that the fraternities decided on their own dissolution. In the army of the German Republic, in 1920, to cite another example, more than 60 per cent of the general officers were of aristocratic birth; in the army of the Third Reich, in 1939, well over 70 per cent of all general officers had last names that did not begin with "von." A common purpose, and a common ideal of service, were to provide the new social order. "We do not want a state," one young writer told an enthusiastic student audience in 1933, "we want a national community."

Both the selections that follow have deliberately been taken from sources that appeared after 1945, lest they be suspected of being propagandist or self-serving. The first is from a book by Milton Mayer, an American Quaker of Jewish background who in the 1950's conducted a long series of interviews with a group of former Nazis in a small town in Hesse. The second comes from the memoirs of Melita Maschmann, born in 1918, once a convinced National Socialist and press secretary in the official Youth Organization, who later came to see the criminality as well as the mendacity of the ideology she had once believed in.

. . . Heinrich Hildebrandt joined the Party in 1937. . . . He had been an anti-Nazi, an active moderate democrat in East Prussia before he came quietly to Hesse in 1935 and, his past uneasily buried, got a job teaching literature and French in the Kronenberg Realgymnasium, the humanistic high school. An anti-Nazi and a cultivated man, more clearly aware than most men of the primitive considerations which directed his course of action—and yet he, too, once he was inside the system he hated, sheep that he was in wolf's clothing, found something profoundly good in it.

"Perhaps," he said, "it was because I wanted, unconsciously, to justify what I had done. If so, I succeeded. But I say it now, too, and I know it now. There were good things, great things, in the system—and the system itself was evil."

"For instance?"

"You mean about the evils?"

"No, I know about those. About 'the good things, the great things.' "

"Perhaps I should make it singular instead of plural, the good thing. For the first time in my life I was really the peer of men who, in the Kaiser time and in the Weimar time, had always belonged to classes lower or higher than my own, men whom one had always looked down on or up to, but never at. In the Labor Front—I represented the teachers' association—I came to know such people at first hand, to know their lives and to have them know mine. Even in America— perhaps; I have never been there—I suspect that the teacher who talks about 'the common people' has never known one, really known one, not even if he himself came from among them, as I, with an Army officer as a father, did not. National Socialism broke down that separation, that class distinction. Democracy—such democracy as we had had —didn't do it and is not doing it now." . . .

Mayer, *They Thought They Were Free,* pp. 104–5.

. . . During the Eichmann trial, I frequently talked with the 17-year-old daughter of a Hitler Youth comrade, a pilot who had been shot down shortly before the end of the war. One day, the girl asked me about the special characteristics of her father, who had been a friend of mine. I drew a truthful picture for her, of a person gifted with a sense of humor, and a readiness to help others, a man who was somewhat lazy and lacked, let us say, the pedant's sense of order, but who was a thoroughly decent person, with a special sympathy for animals.

"And he was a real Nazi?" the girl asked me.

"Yes," I replied, "he was a convinced National Socialist."

"But didn't you say that he was a thoroughly decent man, and a helpful one?"

For those young people who secretly look at their parents with the question "You were a Nazi, weren't you?" there are contradictions here that we should not just ignore.

The problem which the question faced me with was this: Should I have told the girl: Look, you and your friends have a one-sided view of things. National Socialism was not as atrocious and abysmally evil as the Eichmann trial, let us say, shows it to have been. It had some good tendencies too. What won your father over, for instance, or me, or many others, was that it wished to create a national community, or that it brought us up to make sacrifices for a cause which was not a part of our selfish aims. . . .

Melita Maschmann, *Fazit, Kein Rechtferti-gungsversuch* (Stuttgart, 1963), pp. 217–18.

# ECONOMIC RECOVERY

Feelings of new vitality and new community might be evanescent as well as deceptive. The visible signs of German economic recovery were not. Germany, under the Nazi regime, was overcoming the effects of the Great Depression. It was not propaganda alone that made millions see in Hitler the man who had turned ruin into prosperity. Again, no other set of figures indicates the state of the economy as well as the statistics on employment; nothing is so basic as whether men work or are idle:

AVERAGE ANNUAL UNEMPLOYMENT
FIGURES IN GERMANY, 1932–1938

| Year | Number of Unemployed |
|------|----------------------|
| 1932 | 5,575,500 |
| 1933 | 4,804,400 |
| 1934 | 2,718,300 |
| 1935 | 2,151,000 |
| 1936 | 1,592,700 |
| 1937 | 912,300 |
| 1938 | 429,500 |

Der Grosse Brockhaus (Wiesbaden, 1952), I, 374.

UNEMPLOYMENT IN GERMANY, IN PERCENTILES
OF THE LABOR FORCE

| 1932: | 30.1 |
|-------|------|
| 1938: | 2.1 |

Der Grosse Herder (Freiburg, 1952), I, 524.

## FREEWAYS AND PEOPLE'S CARS

Nor was work created solely by means of absorbing millions into the armed forces, or into the newly created Labor Corps, in which all young Germans had to serve for a six-month period, or into the burgeoning armaments industry. The most notable among the public works projects that served sound peaceful (as well as potential military) functions was that of the *Autobahnen*, the great system of freeways built under Hitler. And at a time when owning an automobile, in Europe, was the prerogative of the very rich, the opportunity to use the new highways was promised to just about every German. In 1938, the government proclaimed its intention of building a car that would sell for 990 marks, or $235 at the then rate of exchange. It was to be a *Volkswagen*, a "people's car." Below is an excerpt from a speech by Robert Ley (1890–1945), leader of the German Labor Front, announcing the project:

> . . . As of August 1 [1938], the great savings program for the People's Car "Strength-Through-Joy" will begin. I herewith proclaim the conditions under which every working person can acquire an automobile.
> 1. Each German, without distinction of class, profession, or property, can become the purchaser of a Volkswagen.
> 2. The minimum weekly payment, insurance included, will be 5 marks. Regular payment of this amount will guarantee, after a period which is yet to be determined, the acquisition of a Volkswagen. The precise period will be determined upon the beginning of production.
> 3. Application for the Volkswagen savings program can be made at any office of the German Labor Front and of "Strength-Through-Joy," where further details can also be obtained. Factories and shops can submit collective orders.
> May a project thus commence whose true proportions we can but surmise today, yet of which we know that it will mean another powerful step forward in the development of the German people. A Volkswagen for every German—let that be our aim. That is what we want to achieve, and what we shall achieve. Will all of you help in that; it shall be our way of saying "thank you" to the Führer. . . .

> *Völkischer Beobachter* (Munich ed.) August 2, 1938, p. 2.

## "STRENGTH-THROUGH-JOY"

The *Volkswagen*'s original name had been the "Strength-Through-Joy Car." The Strength-Through-Joy organization, for all the jokes its name invited, was one of the regime's most popular. It was a branch of the German Labor Front, the official Nazi organization that had replaced the former labor unions outlawed by the Nazis. Strength-Through-Joy offered cheap theater tickets, tried to provide more attractive surroundings in shops and factories, and above all arranged inexpensive vacation trips to places hitherto as inaccessible and exotic to the ordinary German wage earner as the Baltic, the coast of Norway, or the Mediterranean. It ran its own fleet of ships, owned a large resort hotel on the island of Rügen, and provided a week in Norway for $12.50, and two weeks in the Alps for $15.00.

"The *Autobahnen*," a contemporary German writer has suggested "were not 'bad' because Hitler built them. But neither was Hitler 'good' because he also built *Autobahnen*." Very much the same observation applies to these programs. And unlike the *Volkswagen* project, in which not a single car was actually delivered to the prospective buyers (the factory switched to war production soon after it was opened), Strength-Through-Joy offered a genuinely functioning program. The two passages below give an indication of the number of people who benefited from it; both come from books sponsored by the German Labor Front.

> . . . In 1934, 2.1 million people took part in Strength-Through-Joy trips and hikes. In 1935, the number was 5.7 million; in 1936, 7.4 million; in 1937, 9.6 million. This year is the high point so far. In 1938, the incorporation into the German Reich of German-Austria and of the Sudetenland, and the military security measures this necessitated toward a hostile world, made such substantial demands on the German transportation system that the travel programs of Strength-Through-Joy had to limit the number of participants to 9 million. In 1939, events made it necessary to restructure very basically the long-established travel and vacation programs three times. Even so, it was possible to continue the travel program almost undiminished until the beginning of military operations, so that in this past year Strength-Through-Joy was still capable of providing 6 million vacationers with their accustomed vacation trips. In addition to these trips, about a million hikes were organized in the past year. These seldom extended over a week-end, however. One hundred and fifty thousand people traveled to Norway on ships of the Strength-Through-Joy fleet, or took part in the so-called "Round About Italy Tours." Thirty thousand people traveled to Italy by land, to spend their vacation on the Italian Riviera. . . .

> Werner Kahl, *Der deutsche Arbeiter reist*
> (Berlin, 1940), p. 38.

> . . . It is not without interest to select one of the districts and to give a cross section of the work performed by Strength-Through-Joy there. We select the district which covers the area of Berlin. Even if we admit that a major metropolitan area, with all the potential that it has by virtue of its theaters and large auditoriums, offers special advantages for Strength-Through-Joy events, it still remains a powerful organizational achievement if in the first five years of the National Socialist Community Strength-Through-Joy in the district of Greater Berlin alone, 37.6 million people took part in its numerous events. The detailed distribution of the audience is as follows:

Participants:

| | | |
|---:|---|---:|
| 21,146 | Theater performances | 11,507,432 |
| 989 | Concerts | 705,263 |
| 20,527 | Cultural events of diverse descriptions, some arranged by the "After Hours" Office, some by the Office for German Adult Education | 10,518,282 |
| 93 | Exhibits | 2,435,975 |
| 273 | Factory exhibits | 525,621 |
| 61,503 | Guided tours through museums and factories | 2,567,596 |
| 19,060 | Courses and lectures of the German Adult Education Office | 1,009,922 |
| 388 | Sports events | 1,432,596 |
| 178,278 | Gymnastics courses in factories | 3,948,685 |
| 1,196 | Vacation trips and sea voyages | 702,491 |
| 3,499 | Short trips, factory excursions, and weekend trips | 1,007,242 |
| 5,896 | Hikes | 126,292 |
| 1,889 | Trips from other districts to Berlin | 1,158,859 |

This report of a single district's achievements is more than impressive. It probably is the best evidence of how much use a working German will make of the facilities of Strength-Through-Joy if these are made easily accessible to him. What already holds for the nation's capital is that all Berlin's theaters and orchestras will perform for Strength-Through-Joy. . . .

Gerhard Starcke, *Die deutsche Arbeitsfront, Eine Darstellung über Zweck, Leistungen, und Ziele* (Berlin, 1940), p. 169.

## THE MEETINGS

An even larger number of people was reached by the political shows put on by the Nazis. It is easy enough to be appalled by these rallies, in which mass hypnosis took the place of reason, and a pseudoreligious ceremonial was made to serve an ideology that denied the tenets of every established faith. But the meetings served a purpose. To the literally millions of people who held some sort of rank in one of the various Nazi organizations, they gave an opportunity to display the uniform that went with their office, and even to those who did not, and who had to be content with being mere spectators, they offered a sense of belonging, of emotions shared. They also were superbly stage-managed; if nothing else, they were spectacular entertainments. The passage below describes the roll call, at the party's convention in Nuremberg in 1936, of the "political wardens," i.e., of the heads of the various local party groups from the block warden up to the gauleiter.

. . . We have witnessed many great march-pasts and ceremonies. But none of them was more thrilling, and at the same time more inspiring, than yesterday's roll call of the 140,000 political wardens, who were addressed by the Führer at night, on the Zeppelin Meadow which floodlights had made bright as day. It is hardly possible to let words describe the mood and strength of this hour.

Twilight covers the Zeppelin Meadow as we enter the grandstand. It is only on the outer limits of the field that a sea of light envelops the walls formed by the flags of the movement, which extend and shine for miles into the dark evening. Twenty straight columns cut across the square of the Zeppelin Field; they are the 140,000 political wardens, who have formed ranks in rows of twelve. Innumerable swastika flags flutter in the light evening breeze, torn from the darkness by the floodlights, and providing a sharp contrast to the pitch black nocturnal sky. The Zeppelin Field proves to be too small. The stands will not hold the vast stream of people who are moving in without pause.

The students of Castle Bird Song[2] march in. The popular name for them is the bird singers. They are perfectly in step; alignment and general bearing are flawless. Then these very best of the party's new generation take up their position in front of the grandstand.

A distant roar becomes stronger and comes even closer. The Führer is there! Reich Organizational Leader Dr. Ley[3] gives him the report on the men who are standing in parade formation. And then, a great surprise, One among many. As Adolf Hitler is entering the Zeppelin Field, 150 floodlights of the Air Force blaze up. They are distributed around the entire square, and cut into the night, erecting a canopy of light in the midst of darkness. For a moment, all is deathly quiet. The surprise still is too great. Nothing like it has ever been seen before. The wide field resembles a powerful Gothic cathedral made of light. Bluish-violet shine the floodlights, and between their cone of light hangs the dark cloth of night. One hundred and forty thousand people—for it must be that many who are assembled here—cannot tear their eyes away from the sight. Are we dreaming, or is it real? Is it possible to imagine a thing like that? A cathedral of light? They do not have much time to pursue such thoughts, for a new spectacle is awaiting them. It is perhaps even more beautiful and compelling for those whose senses can embrace it.

[2] *Ordensburg Vogelsang;* these castles, named and patterned after those of the medieval Teutonic order, were élite schools for training future Nazi leaders.
[3] In addition to heading the German Labor Front, Robert Ley was the organizational director of the Nazi party.

*Dr. Ley reports the march-in of the colors. Nothing is to be seen yet. But then they emerge from the black night—over there, on the southern edge. Seven columns of flags pour into the spaces between the ranks. You cannot see the people, you do not recognize the bearers of the flags. All you can see is an undulating stream, red and broad, its surface sparkling with gold and silver, which slowly comes closer like fiery lava. You sense the dynamics contained in this slow approach, and receive a small impression of the meaning of these sacred symbols. Twenty-five thousand flags, that means 25,000 local, district, and factory groups all over the nation who are gathered around this flag. Every one of these flag bearers is ready to give his life in the defense of every one of these pieces of cloth. There is not one among them to whom this flag is not the final command and the highest obligation.*

*The last flag has entered the field. The 140,000 are submerged in a sea of glistening tips, which resemble a dense abatis; to penetrate it can bring nothing but death.*

*The song that contains the oath rises up into the infinite cone of light. It is sung by the Castle students. It is like a great devotion, for which we are all met here, to collect new strength. Yes, that is what it is. A devotional hour of the Movement is being held here, is protected by a sea of light against the darkness outside.*

*The men's arms are lifted in salute, which at this moment goes out to the dead of the Movement and of the War. Then the flags are raised again.*

*Dr. Ley speaks: "We believe in a Lord God, who directs us and guides us, and who has sent to us you, My Führer." These are the final words of the Reich Organizational Leader; they are underlined by the applause that rises from the 150,000 spectators and that lasts for minutes. . . .*

*Niederelbisches Tageblatt.* September 12, 1936, in Hans-Jochen Gamm, *Der braune Kult* (Hamburg, 1962), pp. 55–56.

## "THE GEORGE WASHINGTON OF GERMANY . . .": A FOREIGNER APPRAISES THE THIRD REICH

At just about the time of the meeting described, in the fall of 1936, David Lloyd George, Liberal Member of Parliament for well over half a century, and British Prime Minister from 1916 to 1922, visited Germany. He traveled around the country for three weeks, and on September 4 had a meeting with Hitler that lasted for several hours. On the journey home, the man who had done as much as any single individual to defeat Imperial Germany in World War I wrote an article that summed up his impressions of Hitler and his Germany. The first draft, as a biographer noted, "was so enthusiastic in praise of Hitler and all his works that the combined pressure of his fellow travellers had to be brought to bear on him to tone down his superlatives." [4]

Superlatives or not, these were the opinions that many people, Germans and foreigners alike, were forming of the National Socialist regime in the Thirties.

## "I Talked to Hitler"

### by the Right Honorable

#### DAVID LLOYD GEORGE

I have just returned from a visit to Germany. In so short a time one can only form impressions or at least check impressions which years of distant observation through the telescope of the Press and constant inquiry from those who have seen things at a closer range had already made on one's mind.

I have now seen the famous German Leader and also something of the great change he has effected.

Whatever one may think of his methods—and they are certainly not those of a parliamentary country—there can be no doubt that he has achieved a marvellous transformation in the spirit of the people, in their attitude towards each other, and in their social and economic outlook.

He rightly claimed at Nuremberg that in four years his movement has made a new Germany.

It is not the Germany of the first decade that followed the war—broken, dejected, and bowed down with a sense of apprehension and impotence. It is now full of hope and confidence, and of a renewed sense of determination to lead its own life without interference from any influence outside its own frontiers.

There is for the first time since the war a general sense of security. The people are more cheerful. There is a greater sense of general gaiety of spirit throughout the land. It is a happier Germany. I saw it everywhere, and Englishmen I met during my trip and who knew Germany well were very impressed with the change.

One man has accomplished this miracle. He is a born leader of men. A magnetic, dynamic personality with a single-minded purpose, a resolute will and a dauntless heart.

He is not merely in name but in fact the national Leader. He has made them safe against potential enemies by whom they were surrounded. He is also securing them against that constant dread of starvation which is one of the poignant memories of the last years of the War and the first years of the Peace. Over 700,000 died of sheer hunger in those dark years. You can still see the effect in the physique of those who were born into that bleak world.

The fact that Hitler has rescued his country from the fear of a repetition of that

[4] Thomas Jones, *Lloyd George* (Cambridge, Mass., 1951), p. 247.

period of despair, penury and humiliation has given him unchallenged authority in modern Germany.

As to his popularity, especially among the youth of Germany, there can be no manner of doubt. The old trust him; the young idolise him. It is not the admiration accorded to a popular Leader. It is the worship of a national hero who has saved his country from utter despondency and degradation.

It is true that public criticism of the Government is forbidden in every form. That does not mean that criticism is absent. I have heard the speeches of prominent Nazi orators freely condemned.

But not a word of criticism or of disapproval have I heard of Hitler.

He is as immune from criticism as a king in a monarchical country. He is something more. He is the George Washington of Germany—the man who won for his country independence from all her oppressors.

To those who have not actually seen and sensed the way Hitler reigns over the heart and mind of Germany this description may appear extravagant. All the same, it is the bare truth. This great people will work better, sacrifice more, and, if necessary, fight with greater resolution because Hitler asks them to do so. Those who do not comprehend this central fact cannot judge the present possibilities of modern Germany.

On the other hand, those who imagine that Germany has swung back to its old Imperialist temper cannot have any understanding of the character of the change. The idea of a Germany intimidating Europe with a threat that its irresistible army might march across frontiers forms no part of the new vision.

What Hitler said at Nuremberg is true. The Germans will resist to the death every invader of their own country, but they have no longer the desire themselves to invade any other land.

The leaders of modern Germany know too well that Europe is too formidable a proposition to be overrun and trampled down by any single nation, however powerful may be its armaments. They have learned that lesson in the war.

Hitler fought in the ranks throughout the war, and knows from personal experience what war means. He also knows too well that the odds are even heavier today against an aggressor than they were at that time.

What was then Austria would now be in the main hostile to the ideals of 1914. The Germans are under no illusions about Italy. They also are aware that the Russian Army is in every respect far more efficient than it was in 1914.

The establishment of a German hegemony in Europe which was the aim and dream of the old prewar militarism, is not even on the horizon of Nazism. . . .

*Daily Express* (London), November 17, 1936.

# 6
## PROPAGANDA

*But no amount of genius spent on the creation of propaganda will lead to success if a fundamental principle is not forever kept in mind. Propaganda must confine itself to a very few points, and repeat them endlessly. Here, as with so many things in this world, persistence is the first and foremost condition of success.*

Adolf Hitler, *Mein Kampf.*

*We have put a stop to the idea that it is a part of everybody's civil rights to say whatever he pleases.*

Adolf Hitler, February 22, 1942, in conversation.

## THE PRINCIPLES

One of the ways in which the George Washington of Germany definitely excelled was in persuading millions of people that that was what he was. Propaganda played such a major part first in bringing the Nazis to office, and later in confirming them in power, that it deserves a brief chapter by itself.

The principles of effective mass persuasion had been laid down very early by Hitler in *Mein Kampf*:

> . . . *It is not the task of propaganda to weigh various rights. Rather, it is to stress, to the exclusion of all others, that which it has chosen to represent. Propaganda must not engage in an objective search for the truth (which might equally serve the other side) and then submit it to*

the people with doctrinaire honesty. Rather, it must, unceasingly, serve its own truth. . . .

. . . The great majority of a people does not consist of professors or diplomats. The small amount of knowledge it possesses channels its reactions into the realm of emotion. Here attitudes are either positive or negative. The masses are receptive only to forceful expressions pointing to either the positive or the negative, never to a half-way station between the two. But this emotion-directed attitude also makes for some extraordinary stability. Faith is harder to shake than knowledge. Love is less subject to change than respect. Hatred is more lasting than dislike. And the driving force behind the world's most profound revolutions has at all times been not so much some scholarly insight dominating the masses as it has been the fanaticism which ruled them, and sometimes the hysteria which drove them forward. . . .

Hitler, Mein Kampf, pp. 200 and 371.

## BANNING THE UNDESIRABLE

It had been the superb execution of these principles, it was, above all, Hitler's mastery of the spoken word and his power over the audiences that came to hear him, that did as much as anything to enable the Nazis to destroy the German republic. Once they had done so, they showed no intention of returning their opponent's tolerance. One, traditional, aspect of Nazi propaganda was to make sure that the other side was silenced, although "traditional" is not an entirely proper term, since there were few precedents for the scope of Nazi censorship. A single week's list of books banned or declared undesirable by Dr. Goebbels's Ministry of Propaganda may give some idea of that. A majority of the banned books, it will be noted, were published abroad; precensorship and natural caution on the authors' part made it unnecessary to put too many books published in the Reich on the list.

## Forbidden Books

*The following books were placed on List No. 1 of harmful and undesirable literature:*

1. Karl Wachtelborn, *What Is Life, What Is Nutrition?* House of Folk Medicine, Hellerau near Dresden.
*The author, who shows contempt for the results so far achieved by*

German science and research, particularly in the field of nutrition, gives a number of confused and meaningless definitions of "life." Simple concepts are artificially confused, and suggest the conclusion to the uncritical reader that the food policy and the health leadership of the Reich are misguided.

2. Karl Čapek, War With the Newts. Translated by Julius Mader. Passer, Vienna, 1937.

This is an open and mean attack, on the part of the author in this overly fanciful novel, on the German people and its political philosophy. There is an attempt to ridicule the racial idea, and Germany's defensive battle against the Jews.

3. Ulrich Baumann, Of Swabia's Past, Swabian Customs. Kepplerhaus, Stuttgart.

An attempt is made in this series to identify German folklore with religious endeavors, and to describe ecclesiastical institutions as part of "German customs." At a time when German folklore is being systematically described and analyzed in relation to its special racial characteristics (SS, Reich Food Office, etc.), such obvious folkloristic confusion must be sharply resisted.

4. Walter Nigg, Martin Buber's Way in Our Age. Questions of Modern Religion, Contributions to a Coming Protestantism. Paul Haupt, Berne, 1940.

This book, which is directed against Germany, contains a description of the work and life of the Jew Martin Buber.

5. Dr. Eugen Steinemann, Basic Economics, An Introduction. The New League, Zurich, 1940.

The author takes the position that the class struggle can be ended only by Marxist planning. He accuses the National Socialist economic order of offering nothing beyond "pretty words," and of essentially being a system of state-directed capitalism, for which the workers were paying the price.

## Undesirable Books

The following books were placed on List No. 2 (undesirable for public libraries and for juveniles):

1. P. Struns and Wolf Greif, The Red Devil. Freia, Heidenau, No. 36.

Waste paper, pure and simple. Structure primitive, writing bad.

2. Erich von Voss, See Berlin, Then Go On Probation. A Mystery. Eden, Berlin.

*Offers a picture of the criminal plague and its organization in Berlin which no longer corresponds to the facts. Besides, it gives rise to wrong ideas about the tasks of the police.*

3. Margarete von Sass, *Game of Love*. A Novel. Otto Uhlmann, Berlin.
*Treats the erotic relationship of young girls, just graduated from school, and still minors.*

4. Hanns Zomack, *The Red Diamond*. Eden, Berlin.
*The author disparages his German compatriots in a number of insulting comments by people of an alien race.*

5. Emil Otto, *The Devil's Kitchen*. Eden, Berlin.
*The criminal of this novel is an Italian.*[1] *The book might give strong offense to Italian national consciousness.*

6. A. Spadro, *Careful, Industrial Spies*. Cultural Publications, Berlin.
*Designed to make industrial counterespionage more difficult.*

7. Ilse-Lore Danner, *Susan Makes Her Way*. Max Seyfert Novels, Dresden.
*Describes the seduction of minors, a danger to German youth.*

8. Fritz Schmitt, *Mountain Fate*. Freia, Heidenau.
*Foul comments about Italian mountain guides.*

9. Fritz Sander, *Fight For the City*. Henry Burmester, Bremen.
*The heroes are hoodlums and murderers.*

10. Tami Oefken, *Tina*. E. Kiepenheuer, Berlin.
*Deals with the resettlement, begun before the turn of the century, of the Poles.*

> *Zeitschriften-Dienst*, No. 64 (July 12, 1940), 13–14.


# ". . . THE DECISION OF THE FÜHRER, NO MATTER WHAT IT WILL BE . . .": SOME PRESS INSTRUCTIONS

Negative measures—banning books dealing with Martin Buber or with nonapproved health theories—were only one part of the propa-

---

[1] This was the period of the Nazi-Fascist alliance.

gandists' functions. An even larger one was the positive aspect, that of providing proper slogans and proper guidance to all public communications media. The following selections contain some fairly typical instructions to the German press. The first comes from a secret speech by Hitler to German journalists, reaffirming basic policy. The next two are from Goebbels's propaganda ministry's daily instructions to the press on how to handle certain specific topics. The last is from the weekly instructions to all German periodicals, and went to the printer a few hours before it was clear whether Hitler had decided on war or peace with Poland.

. . . What is necessary is that the press blindly follow the basic principle: The leadership is always right! Gentlemen, we all must claim the privilege of being allowed to make mistakes. Newspaper people aren't exempt from that danger either. But we all can survive only if, as we face the world, we do not put the spotlight on each other's mistakes, but on positive things instead. What this means in other words is that it is essential—without in principle denying the possibility of mistakes or of discussion—that it is essential always to stress the basic correctness of the leadership. That is the decisive point. . . .

Wilhelm Treue, "Rede Hitlers vor der deutschen Presse (10. November 1938)," *Vierteljahreshefte für Zeitgeschichte*, VI, 189.

[*Instruction of October 22, 1936:*] It turns out time and again that news and background stories still appear in the German press which drip with an almost suicidal objectivity, and which are simply irresponsible. What is not desired is newspapers edited in the old Liberalistic spirit. What is desired is that newspapers be brought in line with the basic tenets of building the National Socialist state. It is thus unbearable that Soviet celebrities who are Jews are described as workers, or that when a Soviet-Jewish functionary is dismissed, there is a comment suggesting certain anti-Semitic tendencies [in the Soviet Union], when in reality every show of an anti-Semitic emotion is punished by death. There also has been mention of the heroic attacks, lasting for weeks, of the Asturian miners against Oviedo,[2] when the attackers were really Bolshevik rabble. If such things should happen again, we would have to draw the conclusion that the editor responsible does not conform to the requirement of the Editors' Law,[3] and take the necessary measures

[2] In the Spanish Civil War, which had begun that summer.
[3] Under the terms of that law, passed in October 1933, a newspaper editor had to give proof of both his non-Jewish ancestry and of his political reliability to be admitted to the practice of his profession.

against him. Correspondents abroad cannot, of course, be informed of this, but it is the task of the home office to examine every dispatch carefully.

Walter Hagemann, *Publizistik im Dritten Reich* (Hamburg, 1948), p. 321.

[September 19, 1938:] The London communiqué[4] is to be printed as minor news. There is to be no comment on it. It is utterly superfluous to have several special correspondents go to Godesberg.[5] That Chamberlain carries an umbrella, and that the hotel has a hundred rooms, can be reported by the local correspondent too. Aside from that, nothing is to be carried but the official communiqué. What should be stressed to the exclusion of everything else is the events in the Sudeten area.[6] The newspapers which so far have been shooting with 3 inch guns should remember that there are 8 inch guns too. The many reports of the German Press Agency about new atrocities, murders, and beatings are to be carried in concise, dramatic form, without unnecessary verbiage. What matters is to show what a barbarous nation the Czechs are, and that their state is impossible. Foreign policy is of lesser interest; such items should be carried on the third page. What is important, too, is the topic: Moscow is helping Prague. There are several indications of this: Jamming of Sudeten German broadcasts, Soviet officers in the Czech army, demonstrations against England in Moscow. Under no circumstances must information about border incidents coming from private sources be accepted; these must be coordinated first. The German press, incidentally, has done a splendid job; the Führer has been extraordinarily pleased by the press.

Hagemann, *Publizistik*, p. 367.

## General Instruction No. 674

In the next issue there must be a lead article, featured as prominently as possible, in which the decision of the Führer, no matter what it will be, will be discussed as the only correct one for Germany. . . .

*Zeitschriften-Dienst*, No. 18 (September 1, 1939), 1.

[4] On the Sudeten crisis.
[5] It was here that Hitler was meeting with the British Prime Minister.
[6] The German press had for weeks been carrying stories reporting a variety of picturesque instances of Czech violence against the Sudeten Germans.

## ". . . A TRULY GERMAN,
## POSITIVE HUMOR . . ."

Nazi propaganda did not restrict itself to advertising the achievements of the regime, or to supplying the proper mood for the pursuit of its foreign objectives. The machinery of the propaganda apparatus was placed at the disposal of a very wide variety of Nazi aims, even though it was a part of Goebbels's genius to recognize the fatigue factor involved in an excess of propaganda, and to leave certain areas apparently untouched by his efforts. Thus one will look in vain, in a German commercial movie of the Thirties, for a storm trooper, or for a character in a stage play who as much uses the Hitler salute. This did not mean that Nazi propaganda respected neutral ground; what it did mean was that Dr. Goebbels was as much a master of the subtle and indirect approach as of the blunt one. The following confidential instructions issued by the propaganda ministry to all German periodical editors may give some indication of that, as well as of the range of the ministry's interests:

## Things We Liked

In contrast to stories where a dog is made to appear as an ideal and obvious possession (and as a child substitute), a little story that appeared in a fashion magazine is in some ways a model worth following. It is true that here, too, a childless marriage serves as the point of departure, but the story, in which the wife would like to have a dog, ends by having the couple ask some kennels about prices.

"When we received their answers, we buried the dog even before we had bought it. A dog won't make you happy—it's necessary to be able to afford it, too."

Here, for once, the topic of the dog as a requisite of a young marriage has been treated with some irony. Without being anticanine, it would be desirable to have our magazines deal more frequently with the topic of married couple and child in preference to that of married couple and dog.

Zeitschriften-Dienst, No. 2 (May 16, 1939); Instruction No. 80.

## Not This Way Please

It is easier to show by practical example than by theoretical discussion where the ever necessary consideration of the interests of state and nation has been forgotten.

If—without, for the time being, mentioning names—we give such examples of clumsy editorial work, we do so in order to prevent similar accidents in future.

### A Sad Joke

An illustrated magazine recently ran the following "joke" on its humor page:

> The passengers of an ocean liner are whiling away the time with shipboard games. One gentleman steps up to another and says, "We are having a race now between marrieds and unmarrieds. You are married, aren't you?" "No," says the other, "I only look that way, I am seasick."

A humor magazine had a similar story to offer:

### Quid pro Quo

> First guest at the hunt: "The devil! You nearly hit my wife, Sir!"
> Second guest: "So sorry! Look, why don't you have a shot at mine!"

Even if one is very broad minded, and has a great basic sense of humor, one must be astonished at how these magazines—at a time of our vital and bitterly serious struggle to strengthen the family, and to bring our entire life into line with the policy on population and race—can commit such a blunder.

The Jewish joke must disappear, and be replaced by a truly German, positive humor. A good example of how it can be done was a caricature we recently saw which showed the sufferings of the only bachelor in his block.

*Zeitschriften-Dienst,* No. 1 (May 9, 1939); Instruction No. 32.

# A GOEBBELS SPEECH:
# "DO YOU WANT TOTAL WAR?"

The introduction of an indubitably German sense of humor was a long-term task. For more urgent ones, for massive, immediate, and direct propaganda efforts, the Nazis' favorite means remained (in addition, of course, to the requisite editorial instructions) the public speech. "The world's greatest revolutions have never been directed by a quill," wrote Hitler in *Mein Kampf.* "That force which since time immemorial set in motion great historical avalanches, whether religious or political, has only been the magic of the spoken word."

Hitler had command of that magic—provided he was speaking to a live audience that could respond to him, and was not alone in a broadcasting studio—and so did his Minister of Propaganda. The following excerpt is from a Goebbels speech, in Berlin's Sports Palace, of February 18, 1943. It was given at a time when the war was beginning to go very badly for Germany. The Allies were on the attack in North Africa; and at Stalingrad, the Sixth German Army, after losing more than a quarter of a million men, had surrendered to the Russians. The selection may give an idea both of Goebbels's general talents as a speaker, and of his particular genius for making the absurd sound sensible, and the unpalatable attractive. (The entire speech lasted nearly two and a half hours; when it was over, Goebbels reported being seven pounds lighter.)

. . . Let me, to establish what the truth is, ask a number of questions of you, my fellow Germans, which you must answer me to the best of your knowledge and convictions. When my listeners indicated their spontaneous approval of my demands of January 30, the British press the next day claimed that it had been a propaganda spectacle, and was not representative of the true mood of the German people. Well, to this meeting today I invited a cross section, in the best sense of that word, of the German people. In front of me there sit, row on row, wounded soldiers from the eastern front, men with scarred bodies, with amputated legs or arms, men blinded in action who have come here with their Red Cross nurses, men in the prime of life whose crutches are standing in front of them. In between, I count as many as 50 wearers of the Oak Leaf Cluster and of the Knight's Cross, a splendid delegation from our fighting front. Behind them, there is a block of armaments workers, from Berlin's armored car factory. Behind them, there sit men from the various party organizations, soldiers from our fighting forces, physicians, scientists, artists, engineers, architects, teachers, officials, civil servants from their offices and studies, proud representatives of our intellectual life on all its levels, to whom the country at this time of war owes miracles of inventiveness and human genius. Distributed over the entire auditorium of the Sports Palace I see thousands of German women. Youth is represented, and so is venerable age. No estate, no profession, no age group was overlooked when our invitations went out. Thus I can properly say that facing me is a cross section of the entire German people, at the front and at home. Is that correct?

(At these words of the minister, the audience rise from their seats and a "Yes" coming from thousands of voices fills the Sports Palace.)

Then you, my listeners, are representing the nation at this moment. And it is you whom I would like to ask ten questions. Give me your answers, along with the German people, before the whole world, but particularly before our enemies.

(It is with difficulty only that Dr. Goebbels can make himself heard with the questions that now follow. The crowd is answering each one of his questions with a single roar of approval.)

The British claim that the German nation has lost its faith in victory. I ask you: Do you believe, with the Führer and with us, in the final, total victory of the German people? I ask you: Are you resolved to follow the Führer through thick and thin in the pursuit of victory, even if this should mean the heaviest of contributions on your part?

Second. The British claim that the German nation is tired of the struggle. I ask you: Are you prepared to continue this struggle with grim determination, and undeterred by any circumstance decreed by fate, to continue it with the Führer, as the phalanx of the home front behind our fighting armies, until victory is ours?

Third. The British claim that the Germans are no longer in a mood to accept the ever increasing amount of war work demanded of them by the government. I ask you: Are you, and the German nation, resolved to work ten, twelve, and if need be fourteen or sixteen hours a day, if the Führer should command it, and to give your all for victory?

Fourth. The British claim that the German nation is resisting the government's measures of total war, that what the Germans want is not total war but surrender. I ask you: Do you want total war? Do you want it, if need be, even more total and radical than we are capaple of imagining it today?

Fifth. The British claim that the German nation has lost its confidence in the Führer. I ask you: Is your confidence in the Führer more passionate, more unshakable than ever? Is your readiness to follow him on all his paths, and to do whatever is necessary to bring the war to a successful conclusion, absolute and unlimited?

I ask you my sixth question. Are you prepared henceforth to devote your entire strength to providing the Eastern front with the men and materials it needs to give Bolshevism its mortal blow?

I ask you my seventh question. Do you swear a solemn oath to the fighting front that the country stands behind it, its morale high, and will give it everything necessary to achieve victory?

I ask you my eighth question. Do you, especially you, the women yourselves, want the government to see to it that German women, too, give all their energies to the pursuit of the war, filling jobs wherever possible to free men for action and thus to help their men at the front?

I ask you my ninth question. Do you approve, if necessary, the most radical of measures against a small group of draft-dodgers and black-marketeers, who play peace in the midst of war, and mean to exploit people's sufferings for their own selfish purposes? Do you agree that a person who interferes with the war effort shall lose his head?

As my tenth and last question I ask you: Is it your wish that even in wartime, as the party program commands, equal rights and equal duties shall prevail, that the home front shall give evidence of its solidarity and take the same heavy burdens of war upon its shoulders, and that the burdens be distributed equitably, whether a person be great or small, poor or rich?

I have asked you. You have given me your answers. You are a part of the nation; your response has thus shown the attitude of the German people. You have told our enemies what they must know lest they abandon themselves to illusions and misinformation. . . .

*Frankfurter Zeitung*, February 20, 1943, p. 7.

# 7

## THE CHURCHES

The German bishops have long ago said Yes to the new state, and have not only promised to recognize its authority . . . , but are serving the state with burning love and all our strength.

Bishop Berning, September 21, 1933.

In agreement with the judgment of all truly Christian people in Germany, I must state that we Christians feel this policy of destroying the Jews to be a grave wrong, and one which will have fearful consequences for the German people. To kill without the necessity of war, and without legal judgment, contravenes God's commands even when it has been ordered by authority, and like every conscious violation of God's law, will be avenged, sooner or later.

Bishop Wurm to the Head of Hitler's Chancellery, December 20, 1943.

In response to the suggestion that later generations would not know the religious attitude of the Führer, since he was remaining silent on the topic, he said, "Well, they could." Never, either at a party meeting or at the funeral services for a party member, had he permitted the presence of a clergyman. The Christian-Jewish pestilence probably was approaching its end now.

Alfred Rosenberg's Political Diary, January 1, 1940.

## SAYING YES TO THE NEW STATE:
## THE CATHOLICS

The one area where both propaganda and the state that meant to be total found their limits was that of the Christian churches. There is no call for legends here. Not all churchmen resisted National Socialism. The Nazis' anti-Communist posture, their public insistence that they were defending "positive Christianity," the churches' readiness (shared by every single foreign power as well) to recognize the legitimate authority of the new government, and the simple and understandable desire for religious survival, all made many a clergyman—Catholic and Protestant —cooperate with Nazism. Until the bitter end, chaplains were supplied to the Third Reich's armed forces, and prayers offered for the Führer from Germany's pulpits.

The following two selections typify the initial attitude of many German Catholics. The first is from an article written early in 1933 by the Suffragan Bishop of Freiburg. The second—issued shortly after the Concordat of July 1933 had provided for a wide settlement of differences between the German government and the Vatican—introduced the principle of Aryan ancestry into the Catholic German fraternities. (Other church organizations resisted the principle. It was a difficult one to reconcile, of course, with the personal background of the founders.)

. . . The Catholic people welcomes the National Revolution, because the entire German nation, more than ever before, is reflecting on its own character, is stressing its own values and strengths. The National Movement wants an end to unemployment, wants the economic recovery of the fatherland, and above all, it wants the spiritual renewal of the nation as against the materialistic mood of the age.

The Chancellor's statement to the Reichstag, "The National Government sees both Christian churches as important factors in the maintenance of our national identity, and the unshakable foundations of morality and decency" creates the bridge which obligates the Catholic to cooperate in the reconstruction of the nation. For the longest time, the aims of the government have been those of the Catholic Church, which, on the basis of faith and religion, has been aiming at reviving the nation, root and branch. Catholics rejoice with all their hearts that the German people have recognized the absolute value of a moral revival; hence we so cordially share in the great task of establishing a new order of values in the spirit of Christianity. . . .

Suffragan Dr. Burger, "Unser Wille zur Tat," Zeit und Volk, I, 181, cited in Hans Müller, Katholische Kirche und Nationalsozialismus (Munich, 1963), p. 173.

## Section 1: Aims

Article 1. *The National Association of Catholic German Student Fraternities is an association of German students of the Catholic faith, dedicated to educating its members in the spirit of the National Socialist ideology. . . .*

Article 3. *The National Association consists of fraternities organized at the universities of the area of German settlement. Only men who are German by descent and whose mother tongue is German can become members.*

*Marriage with a non-Aryan woman shall be grounds for expulsion from the Association. . . .*

Constitution of October 8, 1933; Müller,<br>*Katholische Kirche*, pp. 206–207.

## "THE SECOND GO OF THE GERMAN SOUL": THE PROTESTANTS

Cooperation on the part of some German Protestants was even more unqualified and enthusiastic. The Lutheran insistence on obedience to authority, the patriotic traditions of German Protestantism, and a misjudgment—compounded in about equal parts of charity and political innocence—of Nazism's true aims all played their parts here. And no matter what the precise motives, there was formed, in 1933, a group of rabidly pro-Nazi churchmen who called themselves the "German Christians." (A few of the members also referred to themselves as the storm troopers of Jesus Christ.) What they wished to do was to take over the organization of the German Evangelical churches, and to bring Protestantism in line with National Socialism. A public appeal of theirs is printed below. It is followed by a letter from one of their leaders written ten years later, when illusions about church-state relationships should have been rather more difficult to maintain. The part omitted, for reasons of space, emphasizes the same point that is made in the passage printed—the need to establish a new German church.

## Directives of the Church Movement German Christians (Movement for A National Church) in Thuringia

[December 11, 1933]

1. We German Christians believe in our Saviour Jesus Christ, in the power of His cross, and in His resurrection. The life and death of Jesus teach us that the way of struggle also is the way of love and of life.

God's creation has placed us in the community of blood and fate of the German people, and as the bearers of that fate, we are responsible for the nation's future.

Germany is our task, Christ is our strength!

2. The source and the confirmation of our faith is the divine revelation of scripture, and the witness born by the fathers.

The New Testament, to us, is the sacred document of our Lord, the Saviour, and of His Father's kingdom.

The Old Testament, to us, is an example of God's way of educating a people. In our faith it is of value to the extent that it opens our eyes to an understanding of the life, the crucifixion, and the resurrection of our Saviour.

3. As for any other nation, too, the eternal God created for our nation a law that is peculiar to its own kind. It took shape in the Leader Adolf Hitler, and in the National Socialist state created by him.

This law speaks to us from the history of our people, a history grown of blood and soil. It is loyalty to this law which demands of us the battle for honor and freedom.

4. The way to fulfill the German law is the faithful German congregation. In it, Jesus, the Lord, reigns in grace and forgiveness. In it burns the fire of holy sacrifice. In it alone the Saviour confronts the German people, and gives it the strength of faith. From this community of German Christians there shall grow a "German Christian National Church," embracing the entire people in the National Socialist state of Adolf Hitler.

One Nation! One God! One Reich! One Church!

> Joachim Beckmann, ed., *Kirchliches Jahrbuch für die Evangelische Kirche in Deutschland,* 1933–1944 (Gütersloh, 1948), pp. 32–33.

## VICE-PRESIDENT BISHOP JOACHIM HOSSENFELDER

### Minister of the Peace Church

#### Potsdam-Sans Souci
#### Vicarage "By the Green Trellis"
#### Telephone 6394

Potsdam, March 13, 1943

Reich Minister Dr. Goebbels
Reich Leader of SS Himmler
Berlin

My Reich Minister:                                                    My Reich Leader:

In view of the manner in which the religious issue has been developing, allow me, as one of the oldest of former advisers to the party on religious matters, to write these lines to you; men, both of you, specially called to lead the German state. . . .

The leadership of the state is responsible for religion. It has the requisite conscience before God. A political leadership which remains neutral toward a religion either is not yet total, or has ceased to be total.

If the political leadership, correctly recognizing this fact, is not neutral, it has, when we consider our particular German situation, three roads open to it.

1. It can reject the Christian religion and destroy it with all the means at its disposal. This—no matter whether such a process should take decades or moments—would mean the destruction of the moral and spiritual fiber of our people. Seen historically, such a process took place in Russia. It could, because the Russian leadership used the services of Bolshevism, that is of a prophetic, chiliastic philosophy, which is no longer interested in ordering mankind in individual nations.

2. The leadership can accept Christianity in the denominational, dogmatic form in which it is now organized. This, quite aside from the Jewish influence exercised through the Old Testament, would mean the victory of Rome, that is to say the victory of that power which already dug the grave of the First and Second Reich of the Germans.

3. It can affirm the German Reformation of the Christian religion which became visible in the years 1932 and 1933. This Reformation is the second go of the German soul at freeing itself, within the structure of the religion of our people, from Oriental, dogmatic, and hierarchical influences. Like the Reformation of Luther, it, too, is on the right path. The objection that Luther's Reformation destroyed the spiritual unity of our nation is false. What was wrong was the failure of the political leadership at that time. To the degree that it turned away from the Reformation, it handed the leadership of the nation over to the North. The very essence of the German Reformation requires that it have the support of the state. That support, for love's sake, must show its worth in all fields, for with it, the love of a nation for its leadership grows and remains strong.

Heil Hitler!

Your devoted,

s. JOACHIM HOSSENFELDER

Himmler File, Hoover Institution, Box 10, Folder 283.

## "THE LOYALTY OF MY OATH": CATHOLIC RESISTANCE

But there were other voices in both churches, voices that decisively opposed the theories and practices of National Socialism. There also of course—in the churches as elsewhere—were many whose position was anywhere in the broad area between clear affirmation and clear opposition. The significant fact, however, was that the number of dissenters was greater in the churches than elsewhere, and that besides, the churches offered the one place where the dissenter might still have a chance to be heard.

Among the first of Catholic churchmen to speak out was Michael von

Faulhaber (1869–1952), the Cardinal Archbishop of Munich. In 1933, he delivered a series of Advent sermons on "The Jewish, the Christian, and the Germanic," which brought overflow audiences to his church. Like most of the other ecclesiastical opponents of the regime, he was careful to restrict his comments to matters that were defensibly religious in nature. He also qualified his statements about the Jews by saying that he was talking about the Jews of the Old Testament, and that he was commenting on what he considered essential, and not ephemeral, Jewish laws. Yet the words that followed these qualifications were in very plain contrast to Nazi teachings. So was his attack on the new paganism. The crucial passages on both of these topics are translated below.

They are followed by selections from a sermon delivered eight years later by Clemens Count Galen (1878–1946), Bishop of Münster. Galen probably was the most outspoken and courageous of Catholic bishops during the period. He also was one of the few who openly crossed the line from religion to politics.

. . . It is a historical fact that among no other pre-Christian people do we find so many intellectually outstanding men, men who placed their words and their whole personality at the service of their people's religious order, as among the people of the Old Testament. . . .

In particular, human culture and the Christian religion owe to the Old Testament the sublime and pure idea of God, the most biblical part of the bible, of Jehovah revealed, the ever present, the Lord Sabaoth, the Lord of Hosts. We owe to it the revelation of the one and only God, who will have no other gods beside him. We owe to it the revelation of the supernatural, personal God, who from his infinite heights bent down and talked to men through his messengers, who proclaimed his law and demanded obedience to that law. We owe to it the revelation of the God who, in the poetic, nonphilosophical language of the Psalmists, is clothed with honor and majesty, who covered himself with light as with a garment, stretched out the heavens like a curtain, made his angels spirits and the flaming fire his messenger. (Psalms 104: 1–4.) The divine idea is the highest idea of which the spirit of man is capable. . . .

Let no one treat the sacred writings of the Old Covenant with contempt; God's name is in them. Cardinal Manning once said to the Jews: "I would not understand my own religion did I not honor yours." . . .

. . . In the new year, too, anti-Christian forces will attempt to exhume ancient Germanic paganism. A public suggestion has already been made to give the names of the old Teutonic Gods to the three weekdays of Wednesday, Thursday, and Friday, and to call them Woden's Day, Thor's Day, and Freyja's Day. The Calendar of German Labor is offering parents a list of old Germanic first names to take the place of biblical and Christian first names such as John or Henry or Mary that can be found in the conventional calendars. But the majority of the German nation will not betray and deny its Saviour that quickly. We are not ashamed of our Christian names, names that are on our fathers' gravestones, and that remind us of those who are our models and who intercede for us before God. God's grace did not save us from Russian paganism merely to let us drift now into a Germanic paganism. . . .

> Michael Cardinal Faulhaber, *Judentum Christentum Germanentum, Adventspredigten gehalten in St. Michael zu München 1933* (Munich, *c.* 1934), pp. 12, 14–15, 19–20, and 122–123.

. . . "*Justice is the state's foundation.*" We lament, we regard with great concern, the evidence of how this foundation is being shaken today, how justice—that natural and Christian virtue, which is indispensable to the orderly existence of every human society—is not being plainly implemented and maintained for all. It is not only for the sake of the rights of the Church, not only for that of the rights of the human personality, it also is out of love for our nation and out of our profound concern for our country that we beg, ask, demand: Justice! Who is there among us who does not fear for the survival of his home when the foundations are being sapped?

The regular courts have no say over the jurisdiction by decree of the Secret Police. Since none of us know of a way that might give us an impartial control over the measures of the Gestapo—its expulsions, its arrests, its imprisonment of fellow Germans in concentration camps— large groups of Germans have a feeling of being without rights, and what is worse, harbor feelings of cowardly fear. Great harm is being done to the German community in this way.

The obligation of my episcopal office to defend the moral order, and the loyalty to my oath, which I swore before God and the government's representative, to prevent to the best of my ability any harm that might come to the German body politic, impel me, in view of the Gestapo's actions, to say this publicly. . . .

> Cardinal Count Galen, July 13, 1941, in Johann Neuhäusler, *Kreuz und Hakenkreuz* (Munich, 1946), part 2, p. 179.

## RESISTING A MORTAL DANGER: THE PROTESTANTS

In the Catholic case, it was largely individual priests and individual bishops who engaged in opposition. In that of the Protestants, there was, in part as a reaction to the German Christian Movement, a more organized resistance. In 1933, a Confessing Church came into being, to oppose the threatened nazification of the existing church structure. Among its most prominent founding members was Martin Niemöller, pastor in Berlin-Dahlem. The statement that follows, an appeal issued in 1935 to the congregations of Prussia, is one of the great basic documents of the Christian conscience under a modern dictatorship. (One specific comment on the text: the words "honor" and "freedom" in Nazi usage tended to mean national honor and the nation's freedom of action.)

We see our people threatened by a mortal danger. The danger is that of a new religion. By the Lord's command, it is the church's task to see that our people render unto Christ that honor which is due to the judge of the world. The church knows that it will have to account before God if the German people, unwarned, should turn away from Christ.

I. The first commandment reads: "I am the Lord thy God. Thou shalt have no other gods before me." We obey this law by our faith in the one Jesus Christ, crucified and resurrected for our sakes. The new religion is a rebellion against the first commandment.

1. In it, the racial and folkish ideology becomes a myth. In it, blood and race, nationality, honor, and freedom become idols.

2. The faith in an "eternal Germany" demanded by this religion replaces the faith in the eternal kingdom of our Lord and Saviour Jesus Christ.

3. This false faith creates its god in man's image and essence. In it, man honors, justifies, and redeems himself. Such idolatry has nothing in common with positive Christianity. It is the expression of the Anti-Christ.

II. In view of the temptation and the danger of this religion, we must, obedient to our ecclesiastical mission, bear this witness before state and nation:

1. The state receives its sovereignty and power by the command of God, as part of his gracious order. It is this alone which creates and limits human authority. He who would let blood, race, and nationality take the place of God as the creator and master of political authority, undermines the state.

2. Earthly law fails to recognize its heavenly judge and guardian, and the state loses its authority, if it allows itself to be clothed in the dignity of the eternal kingdom, and raises the state's authority to be the highest and ultimate in all fields of life.

3. In obedience and gratitude does the church recognize the authority of the state, which is founded and limited by God's word. Therefore

it must not bow to the claim of totality, binding the individual conscience, which the new religion ascribes to the state. Bound by God's word, the church is obliged, before state and people, to bear witness to the sole kingship of Jesus Christ. He alone can bind and loosen a man's conscience. His is all power in heaven and on earth.

III. By the Lord's command, the church is to teach to one and all the gospel of the grace and the splendor of Jesus Christ.

1. Therefore it must not allow itself to be pushed from the public market-place into some quiet corner of private piety, where, self-satisfied, it would betray its mission.

2. In all its words and actions, it must honor God alone. Hence it must resist the secularization of its customs, the desecration of the Sunday, the de-Christianization of its holy days.

3. The mission given to it by Jesus Christ obliges the church, in its responsibility before this and future generations, to see that youth is instructed in scripture, and educated in its spirit. It must protect its members, baptized in the name of the God of the Holy Trinity, from an ideological and religious instruction which maims and removes the sacred writings of the Old and the New Testament, and preaches a faith in a new myth.

4. The church prays that God's name be hallowed among us, that his kingdom come to us, that his good and gracious will be done in our state and nation too. In its faith in the forgiveness of sins, the church begs the blessings of God—father of Jesus Christ, who has mercy on those who fear him—on nation and government. Hence the church must be certain that its prayers and its offerings of thanksgiving for any authority, which are commanded by God's word, are given in all truth, and do not turn into a religious glorification and consecration of earthly power and events. Every oath is given before God, and places the obligation assumed in it under the responsibility before God. What limits each oath is that God's word alone obliges us without reservations.

Bound by God's word, the church calls its members to willing obedience, service, and sacrifice for state and people. It warns against the surrender to an idolatry which will bring upon us God's wrath and God's judgment. "We are to fear, love, and trust God above all things."

Appeal of the Second Confessing Synod of the Evangelical Church of the Old Prussian Union, Berlin-Dahlem, March 4–5, 1935; Beckmann, *Evangelische Kirche,* pp. 85–86.

## "THE GODS OF OUR ANCESTORS
## LOOKED DIFFERENT": THE NAZIS AND
## THE CHURCHES

Direct public counterattacks gainst the churches on the part of the
Nazis were rare. The Nazi program had endorsed an undefined "positive
Christianity," and Hitler had no desire for a broad and premature confrontation with the churches. What the intrinsic Nazi attitude was, however, is illustrated by the following three selections. The first is by Alfred
Rosenberg (1893–1946), editor of the official Nazi daily, and the man
charged with the supervision of the "intellectual and ideological training
of the National Socialist party." It was written in 1920, and still left some
room for accepting parts of the New Testament while rejecting the Old.
The second, which rather goes beyond that, was written 19 years later. It
appeared in the journal of the SS, the Nazi élite guard, which sometimes
could say in print what other Nazi extremists would only say in private.
The third is from a secret instruction from Martin Bormann, Hitler's
party deputy, to all gauleiters, the party's district leaders.

> . . . It is high time for the stories of Abraham and Jacob, of Laban,
> Joseph, Judah and of the other archcrooks to stop working their mis-
> chief in our churches and schools. It is an utter disgrace that these
> embodiments of a mendacious and deceitful spirit can be represented
> to us as religious models, and even as the intellectual ancestors of Jesus.
> The Christian spirit and the "dirty Jewish" spirit must be separated.
> A sharp cut must be made to divide the Bible into what is Christian
> and what is anti-Christian. . . .

> Alfred Rosenberg, *Die Spur des Juden im
> Wandel der Zeiten* (Munich, 1920), p.
> 162.

## Confusion of the Blood

> . . . Who is there among us who does not, deep in his heart—pro-
> vided he can still feel with his blood—have a profound, a strangely
> haunting sense of shame when, walking through the German country-
> side, before the panorama perhaps of snow-covered Alpine mountain
> tops or in the midst of the somber Westphalian heath, he comes across
> a picture of the crucified Jesus.
> The gods of our ancestors look different. They were men, and had a
> weapon in their hand, symbolizing the attitude to life that is innate to

our race—that of action, that of a man's responsibility for himself. How
different the pale crucified one, expressing, by his passive attitude and
by his decided look of suffering, humility and an extreme of self-sur-
render, both qualities which contradict the basically heroic attitude of
our race. . . .

*Das Schwarze Korps*, June 8, 1939, p. 13.

[July 7, 1941]
## The Relation Between National Socialism and Christianity
(Copy)

National Socialist and Christian concepts are irreconcilable. The
Christian churches build upon man's ignorance, and are endeavoring to
keep the greatest possible number of people in a state of ignorance. For
it is only in this fashion that the churches can maintain their power.
National Socialism, on the other hand, rests on scientific foundations.
Christianity has certain unalterable principles, established nearly two
thousand years ago, which have become petrified into a system of dogma
that is ever further removed from reality. National Socialism, on the
other hand, if it is to fulfill its functions, must forever be brought in
harmony with the latest results of scientific inquiry.

The Christian churches have at all times recognized the dangers that
threaten their existence from the exact discoveries of science. They have
therefore tried to suppress or falsify scientific research by a fraudulent
science, i.e., by theology, and by dogma. Our National Socialist concept
of the world is on a far higher plane than are the ideas of Christianity,
whose essential points have been taken over from the Jews. For that
reason, too, we have no need of Christianity. . . .

When we National Socialists speak of a belief in God, we do not
mean what naïve Christians and their clerical exploiters have in mind—
some anthropoid creature, which sits around somewhere in the spheres.
We instead must open people's eyes to the fact that aside from this
small earth, which matters little in the great universe, there is an
unimaginably large number of other bodies in the universe, innumerable
bodies, which are surrounded as the sun is by planets, and as these
planets, in turn, are surrounded by smaller bodies, the moons. The
power of nature's law which makes these innumerable bodies move in
the universe is what we call the omnipotent force, or God. The claim
that this universal force could care for the fate of each individual, of
each bacillus here on earth, that it might be influenced by so-called
prayers or by other astounding things, rests on a large amount of naïveté
or on profit-minded impertinence.

We National Socialists, on the other hand, demand of ourselves that
we live as naturally as possible, that is to say in accord with the laws of

life. The more precisely we understand and observe the laws of nature and of life and the more we keep to them, the more we correspond to the will of that omnipotent force. The more we understand that will, the greater our successes shall be.

The consequence of the irreconcilability between National Socialist and Christian views is that we must refuse to strengthen existing Christian denominations or to sponsor new ones. It was for this reason that the idea of establishing a Protestant National Church by merging the various Evangelical churches was ultimately rejected, since the Protestant Church is just as hostile to us as the Catholic Church. Any strengthening of the Protestant Church would merely rebound against us. . . .

For the first time in German history, the Führer, by design, holds the total leadership of the nation in his hands. In the party, its organizations, and subsidiaries, the Führer has created an instrument for himself and thus for the German political leadership that makes him independent of the Church. All influences which might impair, or even harm, the leadership exercised by the Führer with the aid of the National Socialist party must be eliminated. More and more, the people must be wrested from the churches and their ministers. It is obvious from their point of view that the churches shall and must resist this loss of power. But never again are the churches to receive any measure of influence over the leadership of the nation. That influence must be broken, completely and forever.

Only the nation's government, and by its order, the party, its organizations, and subsidiaries, have a right to lead the people. Just as the harmful influences of astrologers, fortune-tellers, and other swindlers are being eliminated and suppressed by the state, so all possibility of ecclesiastical influence must be totally removed. Only when that has happened will the nation's leadership exercise its full influence over the individual citizen. Only then will state and nation be secure in their existence for all future times. . . .

s. M. BORMANN

*Trial of the Major War Criminals Before the International Military Tribunal, Nuremburg, 14 November 1945–1 October 1946* (Nuremburg, 1947–1949), Document 075-D, XXXV, 7–13. (The source, hereafter, will be cited as *I.M.T.*)

## "A HAPPY GARDEN . . ."

The leadership, however, was willing to wait. The church controversy was the one major unresolved issue of the Nazi regime. Several hundred clergymen, Protestant and Catholic, did go to concentration camps for individual acts of disobedience, where many of them died of torture or exhaustion. But public confrontations as a rule were avoided, and only in exceptional cases were members of the higher clergy touched. (Among Protestants not so exempt was Bishop Hanns Lilje, but even here Hitler decided that he should live out the war in a concentration camp and not be dealt with until peace had come.) Consideration of German public opinion, and Hitler's respect for the power of the Catholic church structure in particular both played a part here. But Hitler also felt that time was on his side, and that there was no need (the image is his own) to use dynamite.

The excerpt below is from a private Hitler conversation indicating his ideas about the future. It is followed by a diary entry of Hans Frank, the party's legal expert who had become governor of Nazi-occupied Poland—the so-called Government-General—where some of the future had already arrived.

*December 13, 1941, noon*

*The war is going to be over. The last great task of our age will be to solve the church problem. It is only then that the nation will be wholly secure.*

*I do not care about doctrine, but I won't tolerate it if some fat priest concerns himself with things of this earth. The way we must destroy organized mendacity is to make sure the state is absolute master. When I was young, my position was: Dynamite. It was only later that I understood that this sort of thing cannot be rushed. It must rot away like a gangrened member. The point that must be reached is to have the pulpits filled with none but boobs, and the congregations with none but little old women. The healthy young people are with us. . . .*

Picker, *Hitlers Tischgespräche*, p. 154.

*. . . We won't have to concern ourselves with the church. I won't let any churches in here; we won't have any church problem. Maybe the armed forces will have some churches in the Government-General, but civilian German churches there'll be none. So far no one has requested one, either. If a German in future should have some religious needs, let him go home please. We are, you might say, a happy garden here; the problem does not concern us. . . .*

Hans Frank, March 18, 1942; Stanisław Piotrowski, *Dziennik Hansa Franka* (Warsaw, 1956), p. 314.

# 8
## WAR

*Every healthy, unspoiled nation therefore sees the acquisition of new territory not as something useful but as something natural. . . . Some nations, at certain times, have a strong interest in presenting the existing distribution of the world's territory as immutable and binding for the ages, since this works to their benefit. No matter. Other nations will see the existing state of affairs as something no more than human, which at the moment works to their detriment, and which therefore must be changed by every human means. He who would ban this sort of contention from earth for all eternity might possibly do away with the struggle of man against man, but he would also do away with earth's highest force for evolution.*

*Hitler's Second Book* (1928).

*Centuries will pass in history, and all be nameless. But our age will have its name. What is beginning now is Germanism's greatest hour.*

Hans Frank's Diary, June 14, 1940.


## FOREIGN POLICY: THE AIMS

Hitler had two major foreign policy aims. One was immediate and minimal. The other was long-range and maximal. The minimum program provided for the union of German-speaking Austria with the Reich. This was a point to which he was utterly committed, and on which he was entirely inflexible. The larger, much larger, program envisaged a German expansion into eastern Europe that would provide space for

107

generations of German settlers. Here, he was more flexible. Whether he would move with the Poles or against the Poles, for instance, or with the Rumanians or against the Rumanians, were matters he was prepared to leave to the conditions and the opportunities of the moment. What he was firmly resolved on, however, was that the ultimate prize was European Russia, with its wealth of the Crimea and the Ukraine. That aim became as firmly fixed in his mind as union with Austria.

The Austrian policy entailed the risk of war, the eastern policy its near certainty. When Hitler became Chancellor, he hence was ready for many tactical concessions and subterfuges. He made several peace appeals, he stressed Nazi Germany's readiness to compromise, and he told the world time and again that all he wished to do was to correct the more glaring injustices of Versailles. But these were public gestures, and in no essential regard did Hitler's actual policies of the Thirties and Forties substantially deviate from the program he had outlined in the Twenties.

Hitler's "Second Book," cited here, was written in 1928. It was not published at the time, since Hitler, even though he had been equally frank in *Mein Kampf*, thought it better that some of its ideas should not become open knowledge.

> . . . German Austria must return to the great German mother country, but not for any economic reasons. No and no again. Even if, from an economic perspective, this union were to make no difference; yes, even if it were harmful, it would have to take place nonetheless. Common blood belongs in a common Reich. As long as the German people cannot even manage to unite its own sons in a common state, it has no moral right to colonizing activity. Only when the borders of the Reich include every last German, and the ability to assure his food supply no longer exists, will there arise, from the nation's dire need, the moral right to acquire foreign soil and foreign territory. The plow will then become the sword, and from the tears of war will grow posterity's daily bread. . . .
>
> Hitler, *Mein Kampf*, p. 1.

> . . . To demand the borders of 1914 is political nonsense to such degree and consequence that it appears a crime. . . . The borders of 1914 meant nothing to the German nation. . . . We National Socialists, by contrast, must without wavering keep to our foreign policy aim, which is to secure to the German nation the soil and space to which it is entitled on this earth. And this action is the only one which, before God and German generations to come, will justify an investment of blood. Before God, since we have been placed in this world destined to engage in an eternal struggle for our daily bread, as creatures who will not receive anything for nothing and who owe their position as lords of

the earth only to their genius and to the courage with which they will fight for and defend it; before German generations to come, since we will have spilled no citizen's blood which will not allow a thousand others to live in future. The soil, on which in times to come generations of German farmers will be able to procreate strong sons, will sanction risking the lives of the sons of today and will, in future ages, absolve the statesmen responsible—even if the present generation should persecute them—of blood guilt and of national sacrifice. . . .

Hitler, Mein Kampf, pp. 736–40.

. . . Germany resolves to change to a clear, far-sighted policy of expansion. It shall thus turn away from all attempts at world trade and international industrial enterprise, and instead concentrate all its forces on providing our nation with sufficient living space—and thus with a way of life as well—for the next hundred years. Since such space can lie only in the east, the needs of being a naval power recede into the background. It is by means of building a major land power that Germany shall try once again to battle for its interests.

Such an aim will correspond to the highest national as well as racial interests. . . .

Hitlers Zweites Buch, Ein Dokument aus dem Jahr 1928 (Stuttgart, 1961), p. 163.

. . . Thus we National Socialists consciously put an end to the foreign policy of our prewar period. We begin again where things ended six centuries ago. We put a stop to the eternal drive of the Teuton toward Europe's South and West, and cast our eyes to the land in the East. We finally halt the colonial and economic policies of the prewar period, and move on to the territorial policy of the future.

But if we speak of new soil and territory in Europe today, we can think primarily only of Russia and of the subject states bordering it.

Fate itself seems to wish to give us a hint here. By surrendering Russia to Bolshevism, it robbed the Russian people of that intelligence which, in the past, created and safeguarded Russia's existence as a state. For the organization of a Russian state was not the result of the political abilities of Russia's Slavs. Rather, it was a magnificent example of the political creativity of the Germanic element amid an inferior race. In this fashion, many a powerful empire of this world has been built. Inferior nations with Germanic organizers and masters in command have more than once grown into powerful states, and have survived as long as the racial core of the state-creating race remained intact. For centuries, Russia fed on this Teutonic core of its upper, leading strata. Today, this core is almost totally exterminated and destroyed. Its place has been taken by the Jew. But just as it is impossible for the Russian himself, out of his own strength, to rid himself of the Jewish yoke, so it is impossible for the Jew to preserve, in the long run, this mighty empire. He is not a force of organization, but a force of decomposition. The huge empire in the East is ready to collapse. And the end of Jewish rule in Russia will also be the end of Russia as a state. Fate has chosen us to be witness to a catastrophe which will be the most forceful confirmation of the correctness of the folkish theory of race.

Our task, however—the mission of the National Socialist movement —is to make our own people see that its aim for the future will be fulfilled not by the intoxication of a new Alexandrian campaign, but by the steady labor of the German plow, which merely needs to be given land by the sword. . . .

Hitler, Mein Kampf, pp. 742–43.

## FOREIGN POLICY:
## THE CHOICE OF ALLIES

Hitler's foreign aims, based as they were on pseudo-Darwinian visions, might be less than rational. They certainly were novel. But in the pursuit of his aims, Hitler was a perfectly rational man. What he wanted was territory in the east, not world conquest. He had reservations even about fighting France, the traditional enemy of German nationalist politicians. And, above all, he wanted allies for his conquest of the east, and he early explained who these allies would have to be.

> . . . Only when people in Germany will have understood that the German nation's will to life must not wither away in a merely passive defense, only when we have the strength for a final active confrontation with France, and offer a last great decisive battle with some grand German aims indeed, only then will the eternal and basically unfruitful contest between us and France come to an end. What is basic, however, is that Germany truly sees the destruction of France as a means to an end, which is to enable our nation subsequently to expand elsewhere at long last. . . .

Hitler, Mein Kampf, pp. 766–67.

> . . . There can, in the foreseeable future, be only two allies for Germany in Europe: England and Italy. . . .

The struggle which Fascist Italy is waging against the three principal weapons of Jewry (at bottom unconsciously, perhaps, although I do not believe this) are the best signs that, even if indirectly, this power beyond the nations is having its fangs broken. The ban on the secret

Masonic societies, the persecution of the supranational press, and the
permanent damage done to international Marxism on the one side; and
on the other, the steady strengthening of the Fascist concept of the
state will, over the years, allow the Italian government to render increasing service to the interests of the Italian people, without concern for
for the hissing of the Jewish world hydra.

Things in England are more difficult. Here, in this "freest of democ-
racies," there are few limits to Jewish dictation, by way of the control
of public opinion. And yet, here too a constant struggle is taking place
between those who represent the interests of the British state and those
who are doing battle for a Jewish dictatorship of the world. . . .

Hitler, Mein Kampf, pp. 705 and 721.

. . . If, then, we closely examine Germany's diplomatic options,
only two European states are left as valuable and potential allies. They
are Italy and England. Even now, the relationship between Italy and
England is a good one, nor is it, for reasons I mentioned elsewhere,
likely to suffer any setbacks in the near future. This has nothing to do
with mutual sympathies. It rather rests, above all on the Italian side, on
a sensible evaluation of actual power relationships. Also, both states
share a dislike of the boundless, unlimited French hegemony in
Europe. In Italy's case, that is so because its most vital interests are
threatened. In England's, it is because a France that is too powerful
in Europe might be a new threat to Britain's maritime and global
dominion, which even now is no longer unquestioned. . . .

Hitlers Zweites Buch, p. 217.

## THE STAGES OF AGGRESSION:
## REARMAMENT TO DANZIG

With one of these countries, with Italy, Hitler would manage to enter
into a strong alliance after he came to power. With the other, Great
Britain, he would not, though not for lack of offers on his part.

What he did succeed in doing, however, was to prepare his move east.
The general outline of Hitler's foreign policy is familiar. It began with
the repudiation—welcomed overwhelmingly by the German people—of
most of the provisions of Versailles. In 1935, he announced that Germany was rearming, and the year after that, he reoccupied the part of
the Rhineland that had been demilitarized under the terms of Versailles.
Early in 1938 came the occupation of Austria, and in the fall of that year
the crisis over the Sudeten German area of Czechoslovakia. Presented

with the contested area at Munich, he proceeded, in the spring of 1939, to the total destruction of the Czechoslovak Republic, and the establishment of a German "protectorate" over Bohemia and Moravia. In the summer, he moved on to his next confrontation, that with Poland, using the German-speaking city of Danzig and the German territory Poland had acquired at Versailles as an issue.

Until that quarrel, every one of his gains had been achieved by peaceful means. Struggle might be the essence of life, but he had no desire to provoke one he might lose. (The specter of 1914–1918 was forever in his mind, as it was in the minds of others.) Hitler himself, in a speech to Germany's chief commanding officers after war had been declared against Poland, summed up the principal stages of his foreign policy as he saw them, looking back:

> . . . When I came to power in 1933, years of the most difficult of struggle lay behind me. Everything that had existed before was through. I had to reorganize everything, from the people itself to the armed forces. First came domestic reorganization, the removal of the symptoms of decay and defeatism, an education to heroism. While engaged in that reorganization, I dealt with the second task: freeing Germany from its international bonds. Two special characteristics must be stressed here: quitting the League of Nations and saying No to the Disarmament Conference.[1] It was a difficult decision. The number of prophets who said that an [Allied] occupation of the Rhineland would be the result was very large; the number of believers was very small. I went ahead, backed by a nation that was solidly behind me. Then the order to rearm. Here, too, there were many prophets who foresaw disaster, and only a few believers. There followed, in 1935, the reintroduction of universal military service. After that, the demilitarization [sic] of the Rhineland. That, too, was something that no one at first thought possible. The number of those who believed in me was very small. Then we started building fortifications all around, particularly in the West.
>
> A year later came Austria. That step, too, was considered very risky. It resulted in a major strengthening of the Reich. The next step was Bohemia, Moravia, and Poland. But that step could not be taken all at once. First the western fortifications had to be completed. It was not possible to achieve what I wanted in one fell swoop. From the first moment it was clear to me that I could not content myself with Sudeten German territory. That was a partial solution only. The decision to move into Bohemia had been made. Then came the establishment of the Protectorate, and thus the basis for conquering Poland. . . .
>
> One will reproach me and say: struggle, and struggle again. I see

[1] In October 1933, having left the League, the Germans also walked out of the 60-nation Disarmament Conference at Geneva.

struggle as the fate of all living creatures. No one can escape it, unless
he wishes to be defeated. The increasing numbers of our people require
a larger amount of space. It was my aim to bring about a more sensible
relation between population and space. That must be the struggle's
starting point. No nation can escape the solution of that task. If it does,
it must degenerate and slowly become extinct. That is the lesson of
history. . . .

> Hitler to the Commanders-in-Chief, No-
> vember 23, 1939, I.M.T., Document 789-
> PS; XXVI, 328–29.


## THE PUBLIC FACE: JUSTICE,
## PEACE, AND MODERATION

One major reason for Hitler's six years of unbloody success lay in his
genius for presenting his case. Publicly, he no longer talked either about
the intended conquest of the East or the biological desirability of war.
What he did stress (to a world not overly proud of that treaty) were the
injustices of Versailles and his desire for a genuine European accommo-
dation. Later, when the time for general peace offers had passed, and he
was moving toward the east by way of Austria and Czechoslovakia, he
still did not talk in terms of gaining living space. Instead, his theme was
that of liberating oppressed fellow Germans.

The first selection is from an address Hitler made to the Reichstag in
1933; the second from a public speech he gave at the height of the
Sudeten crisis in 1938:

. . . For every problem that causes unrest today goes back to the
defects of the [Paris] Peace Treaty, which could not manage to solve,
for all time, the most important and decisive questions of the day
thoughtfully, clearly, and reasonably. The treaty offered solutions to
neither the national nor the economic—let alone the legal—interests of
the nations in such a manner that, when faced by reasonable criticism,
they could last for all eternity. It is understandable, therefore, that the
idea of revising the treaty is not only one of its constant aftereffects, but
that its own authors foresaw the need for revision, and hence legally
anchored it in the treaty itself. . . .

That the problems facing us should find a reasonable and definite
solution is in everybody's interest. However, no new European war
could replace today's unsatisfactory state of affairs with a better one.

On the contrary, neither politically nor economically could the application of any sort of force in Europe create conditions that are better than those that exist today. Even if one side should gain an overwhelming success through a new solution by force in Europe, the final result would only be a worse upset in the European balance of power. Thus the seed would have been planted for new animosities and new conflicts. The consequences would be new wars, new victories, new insecurities, and a new economic depression. But the outbreak of such madness without end would have to lead to the collapse of the present social and national order. A Europe engulfed in Communist chaos would precipitate a crisis in the world's development immense in scope and unforeseeable in duration.

It is the profoundly serious wish of Germany's national government to prevent such a development by its sincere and active cooperation. . . .

> Adolf Hitler to the German Reichstag, May 17, 1933; Paul Meier-Benneckenstein, ed., *Dokumente der deutschen Politik* (Berlin, 1935), I, 92 and 95.

. . . There is not much I have to say. I am grateful to Mr. Chamberlain for all his efforts. I assured him that the German people wants nothing but peace. However, I also told him that I cannot retreat from the limits of our patience.

I further told him, and I repeat this here, that once this problem is solved, there will be no territorial problem left for Germany in Europe!

And I further assured him that just as soon as Czecho-Slovakia will have solved its problems—that is to say as soon as the Czechs have reached a settlement with their other minorities that is based on peaceful means and not on oppression—I shall no longer have any interest in the Czech state. And I will guarantee him that! We want no Czechs! (*Applause.*)

> Adolf Hitler in the Berlin Sports Palace, September 26, 1938; *Völkischer Beobachter*, September 27, 1938 (special edition), p. 3.

## MAKING THE INNER VOICE CALL FOR WAR: HITLER AND THE GERMAN PRESS

One of the dangers of this public emphasis on peace was that the wrong people might take it seriously.

"We have heard once more," wrote Walter Lippmann about Hitler's May 1933 Reichstag speech, "through the fog and the din, the hysteria and the animal passions of a great revolution, the authentic voice of a genuinely civilized people. I am not only willing to believe that, but it seems to me that all historical experience compels one to believe it." That was good of course, but Hitler came to fear that his fellow Germans might equally be misled about his true intentions. To meet that threat, he gave a secret address to Germany's leading newspaper editors, in which he said:

. . . Circumstances have forced me to talk for decades about practically nothing but peace. Only by constantly stressing Germany's desire for peace, by dwelling on her peaceful intentions, could I, step by step, gain freedom for the German people. Only thus could I provide it with the arms that in each case were essential before the next step could be taken. It is natural that such peace propaganda, undertaken for decades, has its worrisome aspects too. For the result might easily be that the idea would take hold in many people's heads that the present government was by definition identical with the will and the decision to maintain peace under any circumstances. But that would not only lead to a wrong evaluation of this system. Above all, it would, instead of armoring the German people against coming events, fill it with a spirit of defeatism, which in the long run could not but deprive this regime of its successes. The reason that for years I talked about nothing but peace was that I had to. The necessity now was to bring about a gradual psychological change in the German people, and slowly to make it clear to them that there are things which, if peaceful means fail, must be achieved by force. To do that, however, it was necessary not to praise force as such, but to describe certain foreign events to the German people in such a manner that the people's inner voice slowly began to call for force. That meant describing certain events in such a manner that in the minds of the broad masses the gradual but automatic conviction would take hold: Well, if things cannot be settled peaceably they'll have to be settled by force, but at any rate, they cannot go on like this. That work took months. It was begun according to plan, executed according to plan, and intensified. Many did not understand what was going on, gentlemen, many thought: aren't they exaggerating things? Those were the overbred intellectuals, who have no idea, even when thunder and lightning have started, of how in the final analysis you get a people to be ready to stand up straight. . . .

Wilhelm Treue, "Rede Hitlers vor der deutschen Presse (10. November 1938)" Vierteljahreshefte für Zeitgeschichte, VI, 182–83.

## WAR, 1939

Hitler similarly spelled out his true intentions to his highest military leaders when he decided on war against Poland in 1939. On the face of it, his quarrel with Poland was over his demand for the return of Danzig to Germany, and for an end of the Polish "corridor" that cut through German territory. Both Danzig's status as a free city and the corridor, designed to give Poland access to the sea, had been established at Versailles. He was, said Hitler in public, once more engaged in righting some of that treaty's intolerable wrongs. But he made sure that his closest advisers knew better.

In a sense, matters were indeed going according to the plan which he was outlining to them. He was taking his next major step eastward. In another sense, they were not, for what Hitler wanted in 1939 was war with Poland, not a Second World War. He did realize that Britain and France, since the establishment of the Czech protectorate, were no longer willing to appease him as they had at Munich. The pretense of being engaged only in liberating fellow-Germans could no longer be maintained after his troops had marched into Prague. There now was a British guarantee of Poland's territorial integrity, to reinforce the already existing French-Polish military alliance. But Hitler doubted the West's true willingness to fight. He doubted it particularly since in August 1939, he had successfully neutralized the West's greatest potential ally in the East, the Soviet Union. He had done so by concluding what publicly was called a Russo-German nonaggression pact, and what secretly was an agreement between the two powers on how to share the expected Polish conquests.

In May 1939, he spoke to a small group of ranking German army, navy, and air force officers to make his war aims utterly clear to them. In August, he addressed the commanding officers of the three branches of the armed services to reassure them that the war would be a limited one. (Both selections below, written by officers present, are summaries of what Hitler said rather than stenographic reports.)

*. . . The mass of 80 million people has solved its ideological problems. The economic problems must be solved as well. No German can escape the task of creating the economic prerequisites for that. To solve these problems, courage is needed. We must not evade the solution by adapting ourselves to circumstances. Instead, we must fit the circumstances to our demands. And that is not possible without invading foreign states or attacking foreign property.*

A living space that corresponds to the greatness of a state is the foundation of any power. For a while, you can give in, but then there will have to be a solution, one way or another. The choice is between rise and fall. Fifteen or twenty years from now we will have absolutely no choice but to solve things. No German statesman can dodge the question longer than that.

At the moment, our mood is one of national enthusiasm. Two other states share it with us, Italy and Japan.

The time past has been well used. All steps were logically directed toward our aim.

After six years, the situation today is as follows:

Some minor exceptions aside, Germany is united. There are no further successes to be achieved without bloodshed.

How the borders are drawn is militarily important.

Poland is no additional enemy. Poland will always be on the side of our adversaries. In spite of friendship agreements,[2] the Poles always had the inner intention of exploiting every opportunity against us.

Danzig is not the object at issue. The object is to increase our living space in the East, to secure our food supply, and to solve the problem of the Baltic. To provide sufficient food, you must have sparsely settled areas. This is fertile soil, whose surpluses will be very much increased by German, thorough management.

No other such possibility can be seen in Europe. . . .

> Memorandum by Colonel Schmundt, May 23, 1939; I.M.T., Document 079-L, XXXVII, 548–49.

. . . In the Führer's view, the probability of the Western powers' intervening in the conflict is not great.

Of course, there was great risk involved in implementing his plans. It would be an absolute mistake to assume that the politician had a direct line to God. Nobody expected that from a general, but in a politician's case, that was what people hoped. But it was no more true of the politician than of the general. Both had found their decisions in their own hearts. But our only alternative was either to act, or, in the long run, to be destroyed.

He, the Führer, might say that in judging crisis situations so far, he had been right. Might he remind his listeners of our quitting the League and of our introduction of universal military service. . . . Might he remind them of the Rhineland occupation. . . .

The attitude of England toward Poland can be seen from the loan negotiations. England had turned down Poland's request for 8 million in gold, even though the British had poured half a billion into China. When Poland then asked for arms, they gave them ludicrous amounts

---

[2] In 1934, Hitler had concluded a ten-year nonaggression pact with Poland.

of obsolete *matériel*. In other words, the British had refused any real help, saying that they needed the money and the arms for themselves. All they had been willing to give were credits for purchasing British goods. That was no real help. England, it was clear, was in a precarious situation.

"It therefore seems out of the question to me that in such a situation, a responsible British statesman will assume the risk of war for his country."

France cannot afford a long and bloody war. Its manpower is too small, its supplies are insufficient. France has been pushed into this whole situation against its will; for France, the term war of nerves applies. . . .

> Memorandum, by Admiral Böhm, August
> 22, 1939; Hohlfeld, *Dokumente*, V, 76–78.


## THE WAR EXPANDS


The assumption that the war would be a limited one between Germany and Poland was Hitler's first great diplomatic miscalculation. But there seemed no need to feel contrite. There followed, very much under Hitler's personal direction, a series of brilliant military compaigns that brought not only quick victory over Poland, but mastery over continental Europe as well. Only the defeat of Great Britain eluded Hitler. In that situation he decided, in 1941, to revert to his original plan of conquering Russia.

Later that year, the United States also entered the war, but that was through Japan's, not Germany's choice. Hitler would clearly have preferred a neutral United States. The Russian invasion, however, was very much his decision; he now was putting the theories of *Mein Kampf* into practice.

The first selection is from an SS brochure explaining the ideological reasons for the war. The second, from a private letter by a 22-year-old German student, is considerably more sober in tone; yet it indicates how responsive people could be to Nazi propaganda.


## *Once More the Goths Are Riding*

. . . That which the Goths, the Varangians, and all the individual migrants of Germanic blood failed to achieve, that we now shall—a new Teutonic migration, brought about by our Leader, the Leader of all Teutons. Now we shall beat back the storm of the steppe, now we shall finally secure Europe's eastern frontier. Now there will be fulfilled what Germanic fighters once dreamt of in the forests and vastnesses of the East. A 3000-year-old chapter of history today reaches its glorious conclusion. Once again, since June 1942, the Goths are riding—each one of us a Teutonic fighter! . . .

> SS Leitheft; in Walther Hofer, *Der Nationalsozialismus, Dokumente 1933–1945* (Frankfurt, 1957), p. 250.

> At the front, June 22, 1941
> Sunday morning, at 11:00

My dear ones:

You know what the hour has struck. In today's early morning hours, the fight against Russia began, the struggle of young Europe against the greater part of Asia. Our position is still 15 miles from the river Bug, but we are prepared for action. In the distance, you can hear the muffled rumbles of the front, planes are flying overhead, and we lie in the sunlit grass under high trees and wait for our call. So once again, we won't be in the first wave, but we do believe that we will be needed in the next few days. Last night, the first lieutenant read the Führer's proclamation to us, and this time, we finally are likely to have a chance to do our share. I don't want the quiet hours that are still left to us to pass without sending this greeting to you, even though I don't know when I'll be able to send it off. . . .

> Walter and Hans Bähr, eds., *Kriegsbriefe gefallener Studenten 1939–1945* (Tübingen, 1952), p. 51.

## THE SOLDIERS' WAR,
### 1939–1945

Not everyone was this convinced. The following four letters, all written by young Germans who died in action, indicate some of the varying attitudes toward the war. They were perhaps less characteristic of the prevailing mood than the clear affirmation of the previous letter; yet the positions of reluctant cooperation, powerless opposition, flight into inwardness, and frank recognition of guilt that they reveal are more than the isolated reactions of the individual writers. (The fourth letter is without signature. It was part of the last shipment of mail flown out from the encircled German army at Stalingrad in January 1943. All the letters were opened, the names of writers and addressees removed, and

the contents analyzed by German army intelligence. The results of the
analysis, by the way, were: "A. Positive attitude toward the conduct of
the war, 2.1%. B. Dubious, 4.4%. C. Lacking faith, negative, 57.1%.
D. In opposition, 3.4%. E. No position taken, indifferent, 33%.")

WOLFGANG DÖRING, Ph.D., Tübingen
b. December 10, 1908, in Sande
d. October 9, 1941, near Fjediene, Russia

Modlin [Poland], October 8, 1939

. . . The political events of the last few weeks and months did not
surprise me. They found me prepared. What did shock me, and what
I had not been able to imagine, was the sight of the reality of war in all
its brutality. It is a reality that one cannot and must not adjust to. It
is something so extraordinary and monstrous that one should not absorb it into one's life but let it stay outside as something that can
never be comprehended or assimilated. It is difficult to find the right
attitude—neither to become soft and be overwhelmed by it all, nor
to harden oneself and be too tough and unfeeling to see the truth. Both
reactions are in evidence, the latter unfortunately more so than the
former. . . .

LUDWIG MOLLWITZ, Student of theology, Leipzig and Heidelberg
b. May 21, 1916, in Bischheim, Saxony
d. June 17, 1942, during the assault on Cheka fortress near Sevastopol

May 31, 1941

. . . I am grateful for all the news about the "slipping mask." Examples, time and again, of the mocking words of "national good," of
"national feeling," of all those things which supposedly, according to
those special laws of the blood, should flow from our national and
racial soul. And what the words disguise is the arbitrary establishment
and ordering of these things. In our soldiers' existence, we are removed from all this at the moment, and not directly oppressed by it.
But behind our backs, there is another war for our fatherland. . . .

JOACHIM BANNES, Publisher's reader
b. January 24, 1906, in Breslau
d. March 6, 1944, at Monte Fortino, northern Italy

In battle quarters, October 20, 1942

. . . I have been studying Bach's cantatas again, and transcribing
the most beautiful of the choruses for four-handed piano. In accordance
with the philosophical theme which has most profoundly occupied me

over the last year and a half—the idea of death in German intellectual history—I first looked for those cantatas which deal with dying.

And while I try to let my soul be filled with this incomprehensibly great art, and lovingly copy note by note, I think of Stalingrad, and the many comrades out there, who now celebrate their last hour, and who should enter another world with this magnificent music. Thus I am at the same time holding a requiem for the fallen, and forget for an hour the troubles and the tedium of the orderly room, by lifting myself, in my own way, to the ultimates of our present fate. . . .

Bähr and Bähr, *Kriegsbriefe*, pp. 14–16, 117–18, and 304.

[Stalingrad, c. January 1943]

. . . I love you very much, and you love me, and so you are to know the truth. It is in this letter. The truth is the knowledge that this is the grimmest of struggles in a hopeless situation. Misery, hunger, cold, resignation, doubt, despair, and terrible ways of dying. More I will not say about it. I did not talk about it when home on leave, either, nor was there anything about it in my letters. When we were together (and I mean through our letters, too) we were husband and wife, and the war was merely an ugly though necessary accompaniment to our lives. But the truth also is the knowledge that what I wrote above is no plaint and no lament but a statement of objective fact.

I cannot deny my personal share in all this. But it is in a ratio of 1 to 70 million. The ratio is small; still, it is there. I would not think of evading my responsibility and I reason that by giving my life, I have paid my debt. There is no arguing over questions of honor. . . .

"Letzte Briefe aus Stalingrad," *Aus Politik und Zeitgeschichte*. December 28, 1955, p. 795.

## OCCUPATION: THE PRINCIPLES

What the terrible ways of dying were meant to achieve, particularly in Nazi-occupied eastern Europe, was outlined early by Hitler. The first passage was written in 1928. The second is from a conversation held in 1942. Once again, his basic views had not changed.

. . . In truth, the foreign policy of the bourgeois national world has always been a border policy only. The foreign policy of the National Socialist movement, on the other hand, will always be a policy of space. The German bourgeoisie, in its boldest planning, might get so far as to

unite all Germans in one nation, but it will dissipate its strength in
bungling attempts to regulate the frontiers.

The National Socialist movement, by contrast, will always let its
foreign policy be guided by the need to secure the space necessary for
the life of our nation. It knows no Germanizing or assimilation, as the
national bourgeoisie does. All it knows is the spread of our own people.
It will never see a national, let alone a racial gain in a conquered
Czechoslovakia or Poland whose people have, as the phrase goes, been
Germanized. This would be a racial weakening of our people. For the
National Socialist idea of nationality is not determined by previous
patriotic concepts of the state, but by the perception of the racial, the
folkish element. Thus its philosophical starting point is very different
from that of the bourgeois world. . . .

*Hitlers Zweites Buch*, pp. 78–79.

May 12, 1942, evening
(Wolf's Lair)[3]

. . . It was his [Hitler's] firm resolve that all the sins which Prussia
had committed in this area would have to be undone in a decade of
eastern work. In ten years, he would demand that his gauleiters report
to him that the eastern territories were entirely German. . . .

The ultimate aim of his eastern policy was to open up an area of
settlement in this territory for about a hundred million Germanic
people. Everything would have to be done, and done with utter tough-
ness, to make million after million Germans move there. Ten years
from now at the latest, he wished to hear the report that in the eastern
territory reincorporated into Germany or occupied by our troops, there
lived at least 20 million Germans. What might be done to provide the
necessary cultural attractions was shown by the fact that even the Poles
had succeeded in beautifying the inner city of Goths' Port[4] by building
broad and handsome streets. . . .

Picker, *Hitlers Tischgespräche*, p. 330.

## OCCUPATION: SOME PRACTICES

Space was made by a variety of means: by low rations, by shootings,
by expulsions. The population that remained was to be used as a labor
reservoir. The Nazi-occupied western areas—France, the Lowlands, Den-
mark and Norway—suffered too. Any signs of resistance, in particular,

[3] Hitler's field headquarters in East Prussia.
[4] Gotenhafen, the Nazis' new name for Gdynia.

resulted in very brutal Nazi reprisals. But compared with what was happening in the East, theirs still was a bearable sort of occupation. The major atrocities were reserved for the East, for the Slavs. (It was this as much as anything else, by the way, which ultimately helped to lose the war for Hitler. For as Nazi savagery increased, so did the number of Russians, Poles, or Yugoslavs who felt that they had no choice but to resist, either by surreptitious sabotage, or by joining the partisan armies.)

The first two selections below are taken from the diaries of Hans Frank, Governor-General of occupied Poland. The third is from the report of a 1943 speech by Erich Koch (b. 1896), who, under the title of Reich Commissar, governed the German-held Ukraine. The fourth is a brief Himmler instruction to the commandants of all concentration camps, and illustrates, as sharply as any longer document, the difference in attitude toward occupied western and eastern Europe.

### Interview of the Governor-General by the Correspondent of the V[ölkische] B[eobachter], Kleiss, of February 6, 1940

. . . KLEISS: Perhaps it might also be of interest to say something about the difference between the [Czech] Protectorate and the Government-General?

"I can tell you about one graphic difference. In Prague, you would see big red posters, saying that seven Czechs had been shot that day. Well, what I tell myself is this: if we were to put up a poster for every seven Poles executed, the forests of Poland would not be sufficient to supply enough paper for such posters. Yes, we had to take some hard measures. . . ."

Piotrowski, *Dziennik Hansa Franka*, pp. 276–77.

### Meeting of Department Heads Wednesday, November 6, 1940, in the Government Building Beginning of Session 7:05 p.m.

The Governor-General opened the meeting with the following words:

. . . [5] As for the rest, we are not interested in the prosperity of the country. This may be the most difficult thing we have to say. We are not interested, for example, in richer or more secure Poles, or in Poles with more movable property. What we are interested in is establishing German authority in this area. We cannot judge this work by how much individual happiness, as defined by governments of previous centuries, we have secured for the Poles. We will judge it instead by how impossible it will become for Poland ever to rise again. That may sound harsh or cruel, but in the struggle of nations over the thousands and millions of years there can be no other decision. It is evident that only strong and tough characters will be useful in this work. Anyone not fit for it has long since departed from our midst or otherwise left us. Our thinking here is imperial in the grandest style of the ages. The imperialism we are developing here is beyond all comparison with the miserable efforts undertaken by former weak German governments in Africa. . . .

The Führer, day before yesterday, expressly stated that this country next to the Reich must at all costs master the harsh task of coping with the Poles, and that we are free of any obligation to Germanize. The Führer further stated explicitly that we had no obligation to create German conditions of life here, that there was no room for Germanizing efforts. What we have here is a gigantic labor camp, in which everything that possesses any power or independence is in German hands. . . .

Piotrowski, *Dziennik Hansa Franka*, p. 272.

. . . On the matter of dealing with the population, the Reich Commissar [of the Ukraine] in several passages said the following:

1. We are the masters here and must govern harshly but fairly.

2. . I will get everything I can out of this country. I did not come here to bestow blessings, but to help the Führer. The population will have to work, work, and work again. . . . Now some people are upset that the population does not perhaps get enough to eat. The population cannot ask for that. All one has to do is think what our heroes at Stalingrad had to do without. We surely did not come here to distribute manna, but to create the proper conditions for victory.

3. We are a master nation which must consider that racially and biologically, the least German worker is a thousand times more valuable than the local population. . . .

Report of Quartermaster Fähndrich on a meeting of the National Socialist Party in Kiev on March 5, 1943; I.M.T., Document 1130-PS, XXVII, 9–10.

[5] Ellipsis in original source.

SS ECONOMIC AND ADMINISTRATIVE MAIN OFFICE, ORANIENBURG

*April 21, 1942*

. . .
The Reich Leader of the SS and Head of the German Police has ordered that the greasy Polish and Lithuanian priests are to do some real work, that is to say that they can be used for any sort of labor. The German, Dutch, Norwegian, etc. clergymen, however, as before are to be employed in the herb gardens only. . . .

I.M.T., Document 1164-PS, XXVII, 40–41.

## OCCUPATION: THE MATTER OF EDUCATION

One problem raised by the use of Slavic Europe as a labor reservoir was what kind of basic education and welfare services might have to be provided. Hitler strongly advised caution on these points, and so did Heinrich Himmler, whose SS was doing most of the police work in the East.

*March 3, 1942, noon*
[HITLER:] . . . *Above all, we must not unleash the German school-master on the eastern territory. Else we will lose parents and children. We'll lose the whole people, for something learned by rote is useless. The best thing would be to teach them some sort of sign language only. The radio will provide each community with what is good for it —music in unlimited amounts, but no intellectual pursuits. We must allow nothing to appear in print. What response have you ever had there to European civilization? What grew was spiritual anarchism! These people will live most happily when they are left in peace as much as possible. Else you breed your own grimmest enemies. . . .*

*July 22, 1942, evening*
. . . *The Chief said in this connection that somewhere recently he had come across the suggestion to ban the sale and use of contraceptives in the occupied eastern territories. If some idiot should indeed try to put such a ban into effect in the occupied eastern territories, he would shoot him down himself. Considering the natives' profusion of children, it would only suit us if the women and girls there aborted as much*

as possible. Hence one should not just permit a lively trade in contraceptives in the eastern territories but really sponsor it, since we could not have the least interest in an increase of the non-German population. But he imagined that one would have to bring in some Jews if one wished to get such a trade going at a real pace.

He thought the danger that the native population might increase even more rapidly than before was a genuine one. For under German administration, the entire condition of life of the natives could not but improve and become more secure. We therefore, under all circumstances, would have to take precautions against an increase in the non-German population.

If, under these circumstances, we were to provide health services for the non-German population in the occupied eastern services, that would be sheer madness. Inoculations and other such varieties of preventive medicine for the non-German population were out of the question. One would just have to suppress the desire for such health measures among the natives. Hence one might well let the superstition spread among them that inoculations were frightfully dangerous affairs.

What was extraordinarily important, too, was not to produce, by some administrative measure, a feeling of pride or mastery among the native populace. Special care was needed here, for the very opposite of such a feeling was one of the essential prerequisites for our work. For that reason, the non-German population must by no means be granted any higher education. Were we to make that mistake, we ourselves would be breeding a future resistance to our rule. One would have to give them some schools, for which those who were attending them would have to pay. But at those schools they should not be allowed to learn any more than, at the most, the meaning of traffic signals. By and large, it would be enough to teach in geography that Germany's capital was called Berlin, and that everyone should visit it once in his life. Beyond it would be enough to have the natives, the Ukrainians, for instance, learn to read and write a little German. There was no need for any instruction in arithmetic and subjects like that.

In this whole matter of schooling for the non-German population, too, one should never forget to apply the same methods in the occupied eastern territories which the British had used in the colonies. This whole fuss about education, which began with the arrival on the scene of those German priests, therefore was nonsense. General Jodl [6] hence was entirely right when he objected to a poster which, in Ukrainian, forbade crossing a railroad right-of-way. Whether one native more or less was being run over surely made no difference to us. . . .

Picker, *Hitlers Tischgespräche*, pp. 190, and 469–70.

[6] Chief of operations of the German armed forces.

## Some Thoughts About Dealing With Those
## of an Alien Race in the East

. . . A basic question in solving all these questions is that of schooling, and thus of investigating and sifting the young. For the non-
German population of the East there must be no school higher than
the four-grade elementary school. The aim of such an elementary school
must merely be this:

Simple arithmetic up to no more than 500; writing one's own name;
the lesson that it is a divine command to be obedient to the Germans,
and to be honest, hard-working, and good. I do not think that reading
is required.

That school aside, there must be no schools at all in the East. Parents who wish to provide a better education for their children, first in
elementary school and then in more advanced education, will have to
make an application to this effect with the ranking SS and police
leaders. The primary consideration which will decide the application
will be whether the child is racially immaculate and conforms to our
standards. If we agree that the child is of our blood, the parents shall
be told that the child will go to school in Germany, and stay there.

No matter how cruel and tragic each individual case might be, this
method—if one rejects, out of profound conviction, the Bolshevik
method of physically exterminating a people as being un-Germanic
and impossible—is still the kindest and best. . . .

> Heinrich Himmler memorandum, May
> 1940, in Helmut Krausnick, "Denkschrift
> Himmlers," *Vierteljahreshefte für Zeitge-
> schichte*, V, 197.

## OCCUPATION: HITLER
## PLANS THE FUTURE

Hitler's visions of the peace to come were extensions of these wartime
policies. There were to be even more population transfers; the Germans
from the South Tyrol, for instance, were to be resettled in the Crimea.
And he would make very sure that the Slavs would have no chance of
staging a successful rebellion against German rule. (In considering these
plans, it may be useful to keep in mind how many of Hitler's wilder
schemes of the Twenties had become realities in the Forties.)

*July 2, 1942, evening*

. . . Moving the South Tyroleans to the Crimea would offer neither physical nor psychological difficulties. All they had to do was travel down a German river, the Danube, and there they'd be. . . .

*September 8 and 9, 1941, night*

(In settling the Russian space)[7] the "Reich Farmers" are to live in extraordinarily beautiful settlements. The German offices and authorities are to have splendid buildings, the governors are to have palaces. Around those offices we'll build those things that are necessary to maintain life. The cities will be surrounded, in a perimeter of about 20 to 25 miles, with handsome villages, connected by the best of roads. Beyond that will come the other world, in which we'll let the Russians live as they please. Just that we'll be their masters. Then, in case of revolution, all we'll have to do is drop a few bombs on their cities and the affair will be over. Once a year, we'll conduct a troop of Kirghezes through Berlin and fill their imaginations with some idea of the power and greatness of its monuments. . . .

Picker, *Hitlers Tischgespräche*, pp. 143 and 429.

# THE WAR ENDS (1944–1945)

What kept these plans from being put into practice was that, by the middle of 1944 at the latest, the war was irrevocably lost for Germany. Italy, Germany's principal ally, was out of the war. The western allies were landing in France. The Russians were pursuing the Germans all along the eastern front. Allied air raids were destroying the cities of Germany. Yet Hitler fought on.

The passage from the U.S. Strategic Bombing Survey gives a general idea of what the air war meant even in this last prenuclear stage. It is followed by a selection from a speech given by Himmler before a group of ranking party dignitaries in Posen in August 1944, and by a letter from a German student; leaders and led often were speaking a different language now. Half a year after the Posen speech, even Himmler was ready to negotiate peace before everything lay in ruins; Hitler was not, and his testament, written as the Russians were closing in on Berlin, suggests how, to the very last, neither his approach nor his aims had changed.

[7] Parentheses in original.

## Physical Damage from Bombing

. . . For residential areas, . . . fire was the chief cause of the damage that resulted from bombing. In many incidents ignition followed the use of high-explosive bombs, as, for example, when highly combustible materials were released and then ignited by the hot gases of the explosion, or when electrical equipment was short-circuited, or when stoves and heaters were overturned. In addition, in certain high-temperature, high-pressure processes, the hot liquids and gases ignited spontaneously when released. But the principal weapon for setting fires was the incendiary bomb. This weapon was most effective in causing destruction in city residence areas. When used in industrial attacks the effectiveness varied from good, to fair, to poor.

Many German cities presented partial areas of vast devastation. Perhaps the outstanding example was Hamburg, where a series of attacks in July and August of 1943 destroyed 55 to 60 per cent of the city, did damage in an area of 30 square miles, completely burned out 12.5 square miles, wiped out 300,000 dwelling units, and made 750,000 people homeless. German estimates range from 60,000 to 100,000 persons killed, many of them in shelters where they were reached by carbon-monoxide poisoning. The attacks used both high-explosive and incendiary bombs as it was thought by the Air Forces and later confirmed that the former created road blocks, broke water mains, disrupted communications, opened buildings, broke windows, and displaced roofing. Most important, they kept the fire fighters in shelters until the incendiaries became effective. But, of the total destruction, 75 to 80 per cent was due to fires, particularly to those in which the so-called fire storm phenomenon was observed.

Fire-storms occurred in Hamburg, Kassel, Darmstadt, and Dresden. . . .

> The United States Strategic Bombing Survey, Over-All Report, September 30, 1945 (Washington, 1945), pp. 92–93.

. . . There is no need even to talk about the matter of recapturing the hundreds of thousands or the millions of square kilometers we have lost in the East. Of course we will. Our program is unalterable. It is unalterable that we will push our racial frontiers forward by 300 miles, that we will settle here. It is unalterable that we will found a Teutonic empire. It is unalterable that the 90 million will be joined by the other 30 million Teutons, so that our racial nucleus will be increased to 120 million Teutons. It is unalterable that we will be the power that will establish order in the Balkans and elsewhere in Europe, that economically, politically, and militarily we will discipline and direct the whole nation. It is unalterable that we will fill this area of settlement, that we will establish a garden here in the East in which to breed Teutonic blood; and it is unalterable that we will push a military frontier far into eastern territory. For our grandchildren and great-grandchildren would lose the next war—which will assuredly come again, whether one generation from now or two—unless the air force in the East, why not say it, is stationed in the Urals. . . .

Besides, I find it extraordinarily good that fate is kind enough to us to make things so difficult for us. It welds us together, we are becoming more united than ever. . . . It shows us all our weak points. All those are falling by the wayside whose nerves or health are weak, who can no longer pull their weight. All right, they're cracking up; splendid! That's nature's way of selecting the fit. In the end, as always in the struggle of this world and this nature and this God, there remain those who are stronger. And all of us have but one ambition. It is that when history judges this age and pronounces the dogma that is assured even today—that Adolf Hitler was the greatest Aryan, not just the greatest Teutonic leader—that history will then say about us and the men closest to him: his paladins were loyal, were obedient, were faithful, were steadfast, were worthy of being his comrades, his paladins. Heil Hitler!

(Long and tempestuous applause.)

> "Rede Himmlers vor den Gauleitern am 3.
> August 1944," *Vierteljahreshefte für Zeit-*
> *geschichte,* I, 393–94.

LUISE GÄDEKE, student of liberal arts, Göttingen
b. November 25, 1923 in Siegen
d. September 17, 1944, in an air attack on Siegen

*August 25, 1944*

Oh, dear father, I am trying to say Yes, but I cannot. Always there's that bitter taste again. Everything is hollow, nothing but empty talk, theatrical gestures. The heroic battle of a nation for its ultimate possessions should look different. If the papers can write that this war is being fought for the sheer survival of German men and women, I must ask myself in all seriousness whether wars are fought for that. The Goths facing the Romans at Mount Vesuvius could have survived. Napoleon allowed more than sheer survival to the nations, and so did the Romans see to it that those they conquered survived. Sheer survival the Greeks could have obtained from the Persians, and even the Jews survived in Babylon. Surely sheer survival is no war aim.

College has come to an end. I wish I had spent these four weeks with you, relaxing! Who knows what is going to happen now. Eight years in school, and two in college, and now unskilled labor. Any girl who has held a job since leaving high school has an easier time looking after herself. And what do I do now? Perhaps I ought to report to the Labor Office before they call me. Or should one try about college again after all? Just as long as it's no mass camp, no munitions plant.

Well, for the moment I wish that I might still see you and attend the christening, and that that might calm me. . . .

Bähr, Kriegsbriefe, pp. 375–76.

More than 30 years have now passed since, in 1914, I volunteered my modest abilities in the First World War forced upon Germany. In these three decades, all my thoughts, my actions, and my life were guided by nothing but the love and loyalty I bear for my people. They give me the strength to make the hardest of decisions, decisions which no other mortal before this has had to face. I have exhausted my time, my strength, and my health in these three decades. It is untrue that I or anyone else in Germany wanted war in 1939. It was desired and caused by none but those international statesmen who were of Jewish descent or who were working for Jewish interests. I made too many offers for reducing and limiting armaments, offers which posterity will not be able to deny forever, to be burdened with the responsibility for this war. . . .

After a six-year struggle, which in spite of all reverses will one day be inscribed in the pages of history as the most glorious and most courageous kind of evidence of a nation's will to live, I cannot leave this city which is the capital of the Reich. Since our forces are too small to withstand the enemy's attack on this particular spot, since our resistance has been slowly undermined by creatures whose lack of character is matched by their folly, I wish, by remaining in this city, to join my fate to that which millions of others, too, have taken upon themselves. Besides, I do not wish to fall into the hands of enemies who, for the amusement of their misguided masses, need another spectacle arranged by Jews. I therefore reached the decision to stay in Berlin, and to choose death voluntarily at the moment that I should feel that the residence of the Führer and Chancellor can no longer be defended. . . .

From the sacrifices of our soldiers, and from my own bond with them unto death, in one way or another the seed will rise in German history and there will be a radiant rebirth of the National Socialist movement, and thus there will be established a true racial community. . . .

Adolf Hitler, April 29, 1944; Hans-Adolf<br/>Jacobsen, 1939–1945, Der Zweite Welt-<br/>krieg in Chronik und Dokumenten (Darm-<br/>stadt, 1959), pp. 379–80.

# 9

## EUGENICS

*It would be madness to determine a man's ability by his race, and thus to declare war on the Marxist view of "all men are equal," unless one is ready to draw the ultimate consequences.*

Adolf Hitler, *Mein Kampf.*

## "EUTHANASIA": HITLER'S ORDER

The casualties of the war were twice those of the First World War. Killed in action were some 16 million men; civilian deaths, which can only be estimated, probably exceeded that number. Of the civilian dead, about a million and a half were killed in air raids. Many others fell victim to Hitler's interpretation of eugenics. The war provided an opportunity to eliminate individuals and whole groups considered racially harmful. Thus, substantial numbers of gypsies in Germany were sterilized or gassed. Thus, a program was begun early in the war to murder Germany's mentally ill. A brief letter from Hitler to the Head of his Chancellery and to his personal physician provided the legal basis for that program. It was written in October 1939, but was dated back to the war's first day. It was a perfect example of the *Führerstaat* in action. No formal law was ever passed to authorize a plan in which, ultimately, about a hundred thousand mentally ill persons were to die. The letter was sufficient.

Adolf Hitler                                        *Berlin, September 1, 1939*

*Reichsleiter Bouhler and Dr. Brandt*

are authorized to extend the responsibilities of physicians still to be named in such a manner that patients whose illness, according to the most critical application of human judgment, is incurable, can be granted release by euthanasia.

s. ADOLF HITLER

[Hand-written notation:] Given to me by Bouhler August 27, 1940 s. DR. GÜRTNER [1]

Jacobsen and Jochmann, *Ausgewählte Dokumente*, n. p.

## "EUTHANASIA": STARVATION

The initial stage of implementing Hitler's decision to eliminate the mentally unfit was a relatively unsystematic one. It was that of starvation. The document below was written in September 1940 by a Protestant clergyman, Pastor Braune, who was involved in the administration of a group of church-related mental hospitals. It was addressed to a number of people in authority in Berlin, including members of the Ministry of Justice, who, Braune hoped, might be in a position to help.

. . . Visits to the institutions in Saxony plainly show that the mortality rate is being increased by withholding food. The daily subsistence rate, as I learn from a reliable person, is being reduced to the equivalent of RM 0.22 to 0.24.[2] Since the patients cannot possibly survive on that, they are made to take a drug (paraldehyde) which renders them apathetic. Oral and written reports make it movingly clear how the patients time and again call out "hunger, hunger." Employees and nurses who cannot bear this any more, occasionally use their private means to still some of the hunger. But the result is beyond question. Hundreds have died a quick death in the last few months as a result of these measures.

Nor are just those patients involved here who are absolutely beyond feeling. On the contrary, these are patients who know quite well what is happening, and are watching how many funerals are taking place each day. One report describes the mortal fear of a patient who had an exact presentiment of the fate that is to meet him and his fellow sufferers. . . .

September 7, 1940; Alice Platen-Hallermund, *Die Tötung Geisteskranker in Deutschland* (Frankfurt, 1948), p. 68.

[1] German Minister of Justice.
[2] About nine cents at the then rate.

# AKTION T4: THE SYSTEMATIC PHASE

At the same time, a more organized and systematic program, under the code name of *Aktion T4*, was being prepared. Beginning in October 1939, questionnaires went out to Germany's hospitals and institutions. All patients were to be reported who suffered from schizophrenia, epilepsy, encephalitis, and a number of other diseases. Also to be reported were patients who had been in an institution for more than five years, who were criminally insane, who were not German by nationality, or who were not "of German or kindred blood." Teams of physicians then traveled all over the country to examine the people so reported. After their evaluations were in, the ultimate decision on who should live and who should die was made by a group of medical experts in Berlin—four of them working on each case in theory, though in practice there were often fewer, just as in some instances final decisions were reached without any personal examination. But the basic procedure was that the physician would go over the questionnaire and, where his decision was death, mark a + in red pencil in the square provided for that purpose, and where it was life, a − in blue pencil. (For a while, one of the experts, a man apparently kind in intention but advanced in years, erroneously assumed that + meant life, and so marked several thousand cards in blue pencil. Following this, special instructions were offered at the program's main office in Berlin on the correct use of colored pencils.)

The next phase was to move the patients properly marked + from their institutions to a number of camps and prisons in Germany. There, beginning in the early part of 1940, they were killed. The children were killed mainly by injections, the adults by gassing. The principal institutions involved were Hadamar near Limburg, where about 20,000 were put to death; Castle Grafeneck, Brandenburg Prison, Bernburg in Saxony, Castle Hartheim near Linz, and Sonnenstein in Saxony. In each of these, except for Grafeneck and Brandenburg, which operated only briefly, the killing rate was about the same as in Hadamar.

The first document is a letter from Dr. Fritz Mennecke (1904–1947) to his wife. Mennecke was one of the physicians active in visiting mental hospitals to select patients for extermination. (He was tried in 1946 by a German court, and sentenced to death. The sentence was commuted to life imprisonment, but he died a year later of tuberculosis.) The second passage is from a report, written after the war, of the transfer of some groups of patients. It is followed by a form letter used to notify a patient's relatives that he had been moved to an exterminating institution.

Printed next is a description of a gassing. It should be read with some
caution. It was written some years after the event, and by a person involved in the program. However, there is, for obvious reasons, a shortage
of contemporary or neutral reports, and besides, it does substantially
agree with a number of other recollections, composed independently
of each other. The last selection is a form letter sent to the patient's
family.

Bielefeld, February 2, 1941
Hotel Bielefelder Hof

  . . . First thing this morning, we drove to the local party offices, in
cars supplied by Berlin. There in the presence of the local party leader,
of the district president of Westphalia-South, and of a representative
of the gauleiter, we held a two hour meeting. Afterwards, we and these
gentlemen, and there were now 22 of us in all, drove to Bethel,[3] where
we had another meeting with Pastor Bodelschwingh,[4] his medical su-
perintendent, Dr. Schorsch, and two other Bethel officials. Very inter-
esting!!! The little that remained of the afternoon was spent in inspect-
ing, under Dr. Schorsch's guidance, the cottages that had been assigned
to us by Professor Heyde and Mr. Brack.[5] I am working together with
Dr. Wischer, chief physician at Waldheim.[6]
  I let the concierge at the Kaiserhof take care of the registered letter,
for we started working at Bethel as early as 2:30 p.m. (The trip there
takes 20 minutes by car.) Each group consists of two gentlemen and
two lady helpers. Between 3 and 7 p.m., I produced cards for 22 patients, personal examinations included. That is a very good quota,
which most of the others did not equal. . . .

Your faithful Fritz

Hermann Langbein, . . . wir haben es
getan. Selbstporträts in Tagebüchern und
Briefen (Vienna, 1964), pp. 20–21.

Dr. Morstatt                              Schussenried, September 25, 1945

  . . . Some of the patients who in the beginning probably suspected
that this was some general measure connected with the war, gradually
learned the true meaning of the affair. At any rate, many of them were
gripped by a feeling of something sinister, so that it was difficult to
calm their fears and make them enter the cars. Real resistance there

---

  [3] A mental hospital, one of Germany's best known, founded by Pastor Friedrich
von Bodelschwingh in the late nineteenth century.
  [4] Son of the founder, and director of Bethel.
  [5] Both were physicians prominently involved in the euthanasia program.
  [6] A mental hospital near Leipzig.

was just about none. A part of the patients did not appear to be very much concerned.

For physicians and staff, the transports were a heavy burden to bear, whose aftereffects were bound to be strong in many regards. . . .

> *Die Ermordeten waren schuldig? Amtliche Dokumente der Direction de la Santé Publique der französischen Militärregierung* (Baden-Baden, 1947), pp. 38–39.

Date of postal cancellation

The patient _____ was moved to this institution today. The reasons for the move are war-connected, and in compliance with a directive of the Reich Defense Commissioner.

In case you intend to visit the patient, we suggest that you inquire here beforehand.

Heil Hitler!
(Institution's rubber stamp)

> *Die Ermordeten waren schuldig?*, p. 37.

. . . It was in the strawberry season. That is in June or July [presumably of 1940]. I was part of the staff that accompanied a transport of patients. Usually, we wore civilian clothes. Before the transport started, I was told to put on a physician's white coat, however, so that as far as the patients were concerned, I would appear to be a doctor or a doctor's helper. The members of the transport were told that they were going to be moved. But they were not told where. The transport went to the city of Brandenburg, to the old prison downtown, parts of which had been rebuilt into a crematory, since the prison was empty. During the trip, we had to be careful to see that the busses' white curtains were drawn. On the way, between Berlin and Brandenburg, we stopped in Werder,[7] and everyone got a basket of strawberries, and then we delivered the people in Brandenburg.

We went in with these people. We stayed around, for the SS guards told us, "Why don't you have a look at the show." The people were sorted out, the men in one group, the women in another.

Everyone had to undress completely. The reason they were given was that before being moved to another building, they would have to take a bath and be deloused. All patients had to open their mouths, and an automatic four digit stamp was pressed against their chests. By looking at the numbers, the staff later knew who had gold teeth. In order not to alarm the sick people, physicians gave them a superficial examination. They then were taken into the shower room. When the intended

---

[7] Famous for its orchards.

number of people were inside, the door was locked. At the ceiling, there were installations in the shape of showerheads through which the gas was admitted into the room.

I think that 50 people entered for such a gassing. There were a few young girls among them, and we said to ourselves, "Boy, what a shame." There was only a single door to the room, and you could see through the peephole exactly when all were dead.

About 15 to 20 minutes later, the gas was let out of the room, since it was clear from looking through the peephole than no one was alive any more. Next, by use of the stamped numerals, it was ascertained who the people were who, as the examination had shown, had gold teeth. The dead had their gold teeth broken out. . . .

Bert Honolka, *Die Kreuzelschreiber* (Hamburg, 1961), pp. 46–47.

COUNTY NURSING HOME GRAFENECK

P. O. Box 17
Münsingen
September 24, 1940

Mrs. Marie H. . . .
Berlin . . .
Dear Mrs. H. . . . :

We are sincerely sorry to be compelled to inform you that on September 23, 1940, your husband, Georg H. . . . , who was moved to this institution on September 10, 1940, pursuant to a directive of the Reich Defense Commissioner, died here, suddenly and unexpectedly, of heart failure.

Considering his grave mental illness, life for the deceased had meant torture. Thus you must look upon his death as a release.

Since, at the moment, there is a danger of contagious disease at this institution, the police department ordered the immediate cremation of the body.

We request that you advise us of the name of the cemetery to which we shall have the police authorities send the urn with the mortal remains of the departed. If applicable, confirmation of the acquisition of a vault is to be sent here.

We request that any possible inquiries be made in writing, since by police order, visits are not permitted at the present time due to the risk of contagion.

If we should receive no reply from you within the next two weeks, we will have the urn interred elsewhere and without charge.

*Two death certificates are enclosed. We request that they be kept carefully, in case they need to be submitted for any official purposes.*

Heil Hitler!
[Signature]

Friedrich Zipfel, *Kirchenkampf in Deutschland, 1933–1945* (Berlin, 1965), pp. 503–504.

## A BISHOP PROTESTS

Considering the size of the program, it was inevitable that certain slip-ups would occur, and that total secrecy was impossible to maintain. Thus, one family was sent two urns by mistake, while another was told that the cause of death—in the case of a patient who had had an appendectomy ten years previously—was an infected appendix. Following these and other such unwitting disclosures, several members of the clergy, both Protestant and Catholic, lodged a number of private protests. The most telling protest, however, was a public one. On Sunday, August 3, 1941, the Bishop of Münster in Westphalia, Clemens Count Galen, had this to say in his sermon:

*. . . As I am reliably informed, lists are being made up in the hospitals and nursing homes of Westphalia, too, of those patients who, as so-called "unproductive citizens," are to be moved and soon thereafter killed. The first such transport left the institution of Marienthal near Münster this past week.*

*German men and women! Paragraph 211 of the German legal code still has force of law. It states, "An individual who, acting with premeditation, kills another person shall, if he killed while of sound mind, be punished by death for murder."*

*It probably is to protect the men who, with premeditation, kill those poor, sick people, members of our families, that the patients selected for death are moved from near their homes to a distant institution. Some illness is then given as the cause of death. Since the body is cremated immediately, neither the family nor the criminal investigation department can later discover whether there really was such an illness and what the cause of death was.*

*I have been assured, however, that neither in the Ministry of the Interior nor in the Office of the Reich Leader of Physicians Dr. Conti is there much effort to hide the fact that premeditated killings of large numbers of the mentally ill have already taken place, and that more* are planned for the future. But the German legal code also states in paragraph 139, "A person who receives credible information about an intended crime against life . . .[8] and refrains from informing the authorities or the person endangered at the proper time, is subject to punishment. . . ." [8]

When I heard of the intention to move patients from Marienthal in order to kill them, I preferred charges on July 28 with the District Attorney of the County Court at Münster as well as with the Chief of Police in Münster. I did so by registered letter, which reads as follows:

"According to information reaching me, a large number of patients from the County Mental Hospital near Marienthal in Münster are to be moved, as so-called 'unproductive citizens,' to the hospital at Eichberg in the course of this week. (The date of July 31 is being mentioned.) At Eichberg, they are to be premeditatedly put to death, just as members of similar transports from other institutions were, as is generally believed, so killed.

"Since such an action violates not only divine and natural moral law, but is punishable by death under paragraph 211 of the German legal code, I am preferring charges, as I am obligated to under paragraph 139 of the legal code, and ask that the citizens so threatened be immediately protected by having action taken against the authorities intending their transport and murder, and to inform me of the steps taken."

I have received no information concerning any action on the part of the district attorney's office or of the police. . . .

Neuhäusler, Kreuz und Hakenkreuz, II, 365–66.

## ONE PROGRAM ENDS, ANOTHER CONTINUES

On August 23, 1941, Hitler ordered the program ended. His reasons for doing so are still not entirely clear, but the fact that his decision followed so closely upon Galen's protest may have been more than coincidence. (He could imagine, Hitler said a year later to some intimates, "that a man like Bishop von Galen might realize that once the war was over, he faced a settling of accounts down to the last penny.")

Hitler's decision, however, did not mean a total end to the killing. For one thing, a number of physicians went on with smaller, independent extermination programs of their own, mostly by starvation, though occasionally by drugs. For another, a project begun in the spring of 1941,

[8] Ellipsis in original.

to "comb out" the concentration camps, and exterminate the physically or socially undesirable, continued. The project, whose code name was *Aktion 14 F 13*, was responsible for the deaths of an estimated 20,000 people. Its criteria for selection were even more liberal than before; "anti-German convictions" as well as "strong psychopathic tendencies" might put an individual on the death list. Also, Jews were among its victims. Jews originally had not been considered worthy of euthanasia. This view ultimately changed, and about 2000 Jewish mental patients were gassed, though without the subsequent letter to the next of kin. And in *Aktion 14 F 13*, Jews made a special target for the medical investigators.

The project was managed by the same office that had administered the main euthanasia program, and it employed the same personnel. The following excerpts are from the files of Dr. Mennecke, who was quoted before. The first two are from letters to his wife; the last consists of notes he wrote on the backs of prisoners' photographs.

*Oranienburg*,[9] *April 7, 1941*

Let me still start on my last letter from this first concentration camp period, though I'll bring it along rather than mail it to you.

I just finished the statistical compilation of the prisoners examined by me, 109 of them so far. There'll be another 25–30 tomorrow, and that will finish the job.

I am particularly interested in these examinations because of their value for possible scientific research later, since all these are people with antisocial tendencies—and that to the very highest degree.

Thus I am making lists of my own with all the important data before turning in my forms at Tiergartenstrasse.[10] 84 prisoners still remain to be examined tomorrow morning. Since as of today, there is a third man working with us, Dr. Hebold, staff physician at Eberswalde, each of us will have only about 26 prisoners. I hope that we'll get done early enough. . . .

*Weimar*,[11] *November 30, 1941*

. . . I got no chance to do any reading; all I did was to arrange forms and count them. When I had done this, I realized that I had to phone you one more time tonight, for I won't possibly get through in Buchenwald by Friday, since I am here all by myself. So we'll come back here on Wednesday, December 10, and then we can finish off the rest here Thursday and Friday (Dec. 11 and 12). Then we can

[9] This was one of the oldest of the concentration camps established by the Nazis.
[10] The address of the project's office in Berlin.
[11] The concentration camp of Buchenwald, one of Germany's largest, was located near Weimar.

*spend Sunday, the 14th, together in Fürstenberg or in Neustettin, and on Monday, December 15, work will start in Ravensbrück[12] (together with Schmalenbach, probably). . . .*

*This is the way the results of my work in Buchenwald look so far:*

| Schmalenbach: | | Müller: | |
|---|---|---|---|
| *11–25–41* ....... 79 | | *11–25–41* ....... 63 | |
| *11–26–41* ....... 10 | | *11–26–41* ....... 43 | |
| | — | *11–27–41* .......129 | |
| | 89 | *11–28–41* .......115 | |
| | | *11–29–41* ....... 53 | |
| | | | 403 |

| Mennecke: | | | |
|---|---|---|---|
| *11–25–41* ....... — | | | |
| *11–26–41* ....... 35 | | | |
| *11–27–41* .......181 | | | 89 |
| *11–28–41* .......183 | | | 403 |
| *11–29–41* ....... 71 | | | 470 |
| | 470 | | 962 |

Since we have to process 2000 cases here, I still have 1038 ahead of me. . . .

[Undated notes on photographs]

Schneidhuber, Dorothea Sara,[13] b. March 8, 1881 in Läch

Continuously wrote inflammatory anti-German articles about the religious situation in Germany, which she received from an adviser in the archbishop's office in Munich.
541 Ravensbrück 1819

Stross, Otto Israel, b. September 22, 1900 in Prague, lawyer
22730 Dachau[14]

Strong German-hater, troublemaker.

Lampl, Ernst Israel, b. August 20, 1889 in Brünn, lawyer

Lieutenant (Res.) in the Austro-Hungarian army. Anti-German agitation. Troublemaker.

[12] A concentration camp mainly for women.
[13] In 1938, all Jewish women in Germany were compelled by law to adopt the middle name of Sara, and all Jewish men that of Israel.
[14] This was one of the largest and oldest of concentration camps in Nazi Germany.

Lamensdorf, Margarete Sara, widow, August 16, 1883, Landsberg/
Warthe

Ran housekeeping department in Jewish nurses' home. Sabotaged food
supply. Gave wrong figures on rations.

Capell, Charlotte Sara, Oct. 4, '93, Breslau, divorced, Catholic Jewess
740  Ravensbrück 879

Nurse. Continuous miscegenation. Disguised her Jewish descent by her
Catholicism, hung a crucifix around her neck.

Schönhof, Eugen Israel, lawyer, Sept. 4, '80 in Vienna
Dachau 1938, 6069

Communist shyster. Member of the Red Aid, in Russia in 1927. Strong
German-hater, troublemaker. In the camp: arrogant, impertinent, lazy,
recalcitrant. Since 1901 first lieutenant in the Austro-Hung. army. Reserve lieutenant. At front from beginning of World War to May '15,
then Russian prisoner of war. Promoted to first lieutenant while at
front, to captain while in p.o.w. camp.

Fritz Mennecke, in Langbein, . . . wir
haben es getan, pp. 22, 30–31, and 33–34.

# 10
## THE JEWS

In the year 1918, there was no such thing as organized anti-Semitism. I still remember the difficulties one encountered if one so much as mentioned the word Jew. People either stared at you stupidly or contradicted you violently. Our first efforts at revealing the true enemy to the people appeared to be almost hopeless at the time, and only very slowly did matters take a turn for the better.

Adolf Hitler, *Mein Kampf*.

"Isn't the Jew a human being too?" Of course he is; none of us ever doubted it. All we doubt is that he is a decent human being.

Joseph Goebbels, *Der Angriff*, July 30, 1928.

I have often in my life been a prophet, and usually people laughed at me. . . . Let me be a prophet again today: If international financial Jewry, in Europe and beyond, should succeed in plunging the nations into another world war, the result will not be the Bolshevization of the world and thus the victory of Jewry, but the destruction of the Jewish race in Europe.

Adolf Hitler to the Reichstag, January 30, 1939.

## "THE DEFENSE OF THE GERMAN PEOPLE . . ."

*Aktion 14 F 13* had been a relatively minor operation. With the end of the systematic extermination of the mentally ill, the experience, and

145

much of the staff, of the euthanasia program was becoming available for the next major group of victims.

There were two main stages in the Nazi persecution of the Jews. The first lasted from 1933 to the coming of the war. It was marked by measures of discrimination and humiliation that seemed intolerable at the time. The second began with the war, and was very much intensified after the attack on Russia in 1941. It made the first period look mild by comparison.

It began, in 1933, with some scattered individual acts of violence that were disowned by the government. It continued with the officially directed removal of Jews from positions of influence in German life, with the dismissal of Jews from the civil service, and with the imposition of a restrictive quota system for admission to higher education.

Occasionally, there were protests against the new anti-Semitic policies. The most important of them came from President von Hindenburg. It was answered by Hitler in a letter that displayed all his tactical skill. Here as elsewhere, decent but naïve objectors were facing a man whose cleverness was equal to his determination.

*THE PRESIDENT*                                                *Berlin, April 4, 1933*

*Chancellor Adolf Hitler*
*Berlin*

*Dear Mr. Chancellor:*
*In recent days, a whole number of cases were reported to me in which judges, lawyers, and justice officials who are wounded war veterans, and whose conduct of office has been flawless, were forcibly retired and are to be dismissed because of their Jewish descent.*

*For me personally (and on the day of National Revival, on March 21, I addressed a proclamation to the German people with the express approval of the Government in which I bowed in reverence before the dead of the war, and remembered, in gratitude, the war's widows and orphans, the disabled veterans, and my old comrades at the front) this sort of treatment of Jewish officials, wounded in the war, is quite intolerable. I am convinced, Mr. Chancellor, that you will share this human feeling with me, and I ask you, most cordially and with the utmost urgency, to look into this matter yourself, and to let a uniform solution prevail for all branches of the public services in Germany. As far as my own convictions are concerned, officials, judges, teachers, and lawyers who were wounded in the war, or who served at the front, or whose fathers died in the war, or who lost a son in the war, must—as long as their individual cases do not provide reasons for special treatment—be left in their positions. If they were worthy of fighting and* bleeding for Germany, they must be considered worthy of continuing to serve the fatherland in their professions.

In the conviction that I am not appealing in vain to your comradely sentiments, I am, with friendly regards,

Your devoted,<br>
s. VON HINDENBURG

THE CHANCELLOR                                    Berlin, April 5, 1933

Dear Mr. President:

There are two reasons for the defense of the German people against the inundation of certain professions by the Jews.

The first is the glaring wrong created by the incredible discrimination against the German element that supports the state. For there are a whole number of intellectual professions today—medicine and the law, for instance—where in several places in Germany, in Berlin and elsewhere, the Jews hold up to 80 per cent and more of all positions. At the same time, hundreds of thousands of German intellectuals, including countless war veterans, subsist on unemployment insurance, or are being ruined by finding themselves in some entirely subordinate position.

The second is the great shock to the authority of the state which is being caused by the fact that an entirely alien body, which has never really become one with the German people, and whose talent is primarily a business talent, is pushing its way into government positions and providing the mustard seed of a kind of corruption of whose extent people to this day are not even approximately aware. One of the major reasons why the old Prussian state was such a clean one was that the Jews were granted only a very limited access to the civil service. The officer corps kept itself almost entirely pure. . . .

In a most generous manner, Mr. Field Marshal, you plead the cause of those members of the Jewish people who were once compelled, under the requirements of universal military service, to do their duty in time of war. Mr. Field Marshal, I entirely understand these lofty sentiments of yours. But might I, with the utmost respect, point out that members and adherents of my movement, who were Germans, for years were driven from all government positions, and never mind if they had wives and children, or what they had done in the war. . . . And yet, in appreciation of the chivalrous motives of your sentiments, Mr. Field Marshal, I have already been discussing the preparation of a law with Minister of the Interior Frick which would remove the solution of these questions from individual arbitrariness and subject them to generally applicable legislation. And in these discussions, I directed the Minister of the Interior's attention to those cases where you, Mr. Field Marshal, would like to see exceptions made. The law in question was

discussed in a number of initial meetings last week, and will provide
some consideration for those Jews who either served personally in the
war, or who suffered some loss as a result of the war, or who have other
merits, or who during a long tenure of office gave no cause for com-
plaint. And in general, the first aim of this cleansing process is to restore a certain healthy and natural balance, while the second aim is to
remove those elements from official positions who cannot be entrusted
with matters affecting Germany's survival or destruction. . . .

I beg you, Mr. President, to believe me when I say that I will try,
as much as I can, to do justice to your noble feelings. I understand your
inner motives. And I myself, by the way, frequently suffer from the
harshness of a fate which compels one to make decisions which, as a
human being, one would a thousand times rather avoid.

Work on the law in question will proceed as quickly as possible, and
I am convinced that this matter, too, will then find its best possible
solution.

I am, in sincere and profound respect,

Your ever devoted,

s. ADOLF HITLER

Hubatsch, *Hindenburg und der Staat*, pp.
375–78.

# AHASVER, FEIBISCH, GEDALJA AND JEZABEL: NUREMBERG LAWS TO JEWISH STAR

After Hindenburg's death, in 1934, the pace of the anti-Jewish measures quickened. At the Nuremberg Party Rally in 1935, two major pieces
of legislation affecting the Jews were passed. One deprived them of civic
rights; the other (printed below) introduced the concept of miscegenation into German law. The following year or two saw relative calm; this
was the period of the Olympic Games when many foreigners were visiting Germany. But 1938 brought another quickening of the pace. In
November, a young Polish Jew shot a member of the German embassy
in Paris; in retaliation, many of Germany's synagogues were burned,
some 25,000 Jewish men were sent to concentration camps, and Jews
were no longer permitted to own stores or factories. Even before that,
a decree had been issued restricting Jews to what struck the Nazis as
Jewish first names. It is printed below, together with a selected list of
permitted names. The decree was one in a long line of harassments and
humiliations. Thus Jews were forbidden, between 1938 and 1941, to

enter certain Berlin streets or to attend a concert, to own domestic animals or to drive cars, to obtain the usual wartime rations or to sit on a park bench, to use public transportation or to buy a newspaper. Then, at the end of 1941, most of their remaining property was seized, and an instruction issued compelling them to wear a Star of David in public.

## Law for the Protection of German Blood and German Honor

Realizing that the purity of the German blood is the prerequisite for the continued existence of the German people, and animated by the firm resolve to secure the German nation for all future times, the Reichstag has unanimously passed the following law, which is being proclaimed herewith:

Paragraph 1.
1. Marriages between Jews and citizens of German or kindred blood are hereby forbidden. Marriages performed despite this ban are void, even if, to contravene the law, they were performed abroad.
2. Suits for annulment can be brought only by the district attorney.

Paragraph 2.
Extramarital intercourse between Jews and citizens of German or kindred blood is forbidden.

Paragraph 3.
Jews are not permitted to employ female citizens of German or kindred blood under 45 years of age as domestic help.

Paragraph 4.
1. Jews are not permitted to display the German flag or the national colors.
2. They are, however, permitted to show the Jewish colors. The exercise of this right is protected by the state.

Paragraph 5.
1. Persons violating the restrictions of Par. 1 will be punished by hard labor.
2. Men violating the prohibition of Par. 2 will be punished by prison or hard labor.
3. Persons violating the provisions of Par. 3 or 4 will be punished by a prison term of up to one year and a fine, or by either of these penalties. . . .

Nuremberg, September 15, 1935          The Führer and Chancellor
On the Party Rally of Liberty          s. ADOLF HITLER

                                       The Minister of the Interior
                                       s. FRICK

                                       The Minister of Justice
                                       s. DR. GÜRTNER

                                       The Deputy of the Führer
                                       Minister Without Portfolio
                                       s. R. HESS

                                       Hohlfeld, *Dokumente,* IV, 255–56, and
                                       Jacobsen and Jochmann, *Ausgewählte Dok-*
                                       *umente,* n. p.


## Second Decree Implementing the Law Concerning the Change in Family Names of August 17, 1938

Paragraph 1.
1. Jews may receive only those first names which are listed in the directives of the Ministry of the Interior concerning the use of first names.
2. This provision does not apply to Jews of a foreign nationality.

Paragraph 2.
1. If Jews should bear first names other than those permitted to Jews according to Par. 1, they must, as of January 1, 1939, adopt an additional name. For males, that name shall be Israel, for females Sara.

                                       Jacobsen and Jochmann, *Ausgewählte Dok-*
                                       *umente,* n. p.


. . . In a circular instruction of the Ministry of the Interior, these names were announced as Jewish first names:[1]

Male First Names: Abimelech, Ahasver, Anschel, Bachja, Barak, Baruch, Chaggai, Chajin, Chananja, Denny, Ehud, Eisig, Faleg, Feibisch, Feitel, Gedalja, Hemor, Henoch, Isidor, Itzig, Jakusiel, Jiftach, Jomteb, Kaleb, Korach, Laban, Leiser, Machol, Menachem, Mosche, Moses, Naftali, Nissi, Nochem, Oscher, Pinchas, Pinkus, Rachmiel, Sallum, Salusch, Schalom, Schnur, Teit, Tewele, Uria, Zedek, Zephania.

Female First Names: Abigail, Baile, Breine, Brocha, Chana, Cheiche,

---

[1]The list that follows has been abbreviated to about one fourth its original length. The connotations of the names omitted were similar to those that are given here, however.

Chinke, Deiche, Driesel, Egele, Feigle, Fradchen, Gaugel, Ginendel,
Hadasse, Hitzel, Jachel, Jezabel, Keile, Libsche, Machle, Milkele, Nacha,
Peirche, Pesse, Pessel, Rebekka, Rechel, Reitzsche, Scharne, Scheindel,
Schlaemche, Tana, Treibel, Zilla, Zimle, Zipora.

*Völkischer Beobachter,* August 24, 1938,
p. 2.

## Police Decree Concerning the Marking of Jews of September 1, 1941

Paragraph 1.
1. Jews (see Par. 5 of the First Executive Decree Concerning the
Reich Citizenship Law of November 14, 1935; Official Gazette, p.
1333) over the age of six are forbidden to show themselves in public
without a Jew's star.
2. The Jew's star consists of a six-pointed star of yellow cloth with
black borders, equivalent in size to the palm of the hand. The inscription is to read "JEW" in black letters. It is to be sewn to the left
breast of the garment, and to be worn visibly.

Paragraph 2.
Jews are forbidden
a) to leave their area of residence without carrying, on their person,
   written permission from the local police.
b) to wear medals, decorations, or other insignia. . . .

Hofer, *Der Nationalsozialismus,* p. 297.

## DEPORTATIONS AND SHOOTINGS: THE EXTERMINATION BEGINS

The aim, up to the outbreak of the war, had been to show the correctness of the Nazi view that Jews could not possibly be Germans, and
beyond that, to put every conceivable pressure on the Jews to induce
them to emigrate. And some 300,000 did leave the country in the years
that followed Hitler's accession to power. But by 1941, the possibility
of emigration was closed. Moreover, with their conquest of Poland in
1939, and the invasion of the Baltic states and of Russia two years later,
the Nazis brought many more millions of Jews into their sphere of
influence. Emigration no longer struck them as a feasible solution, even

though a project of shipping all Jews to the island of Madagascar was
considered at least semiseriously for awhile. The over-all aim, then, after
1941, became extermination.

Many of the Jews in the eastern territories were driven into newly
constructed ghettos or concentration camps, with the aim of working
them to death. Many more were shot by special SS squads and their
local volunteer helpers. (Sometimes the method of execution varied.
In Riga, for instance, convicts were released from prison, given iron
bars, and told to kill Jews. But the usual method was mass shootings.)
Toward the end of 1941, the deportation of German Jews to the East
began, to be followed by transports of Jews from the Nazi-occupied
western European nations.

The letter below was written by an employee of the Central Jewish
Congregation in Berlin in January 1942. It is followed by an undated map
accompanying a progress report of a special SS execution squad, which
was very probably submitted at about the same time. The two final
selections are from a report of the Nazi District Commissioner of Slonim
in White Russia, and from that of an SS sergeant.

. . . *Since the beginning of January, three more transports have left
(all of them for Riga) so that 10,000 people are already gone from
Berlin. In February, there will be a pause. To make up for it, it will
probably go on with increased speed in March. But at least it won't be
so cold then. The latest development is that all the evacuees—or, as the
only expression you are allowed to use has it, the "emigrants"—who are
under 60 must walk from Lewetzow Street to Grunewald Station. Can
you imagine what this means during the current cold spell? The people
who left yesterday went in cattle cars. There were very many old people
among them. Some of them, up to the age of 75, were taken from
retirement homes. How many of the old people won't even survive the
trip! What happens afterward, no one knows. Since the beginning of
the year, there has been no more news from Litzmannstadt.[2] Mail sent
there is returned with the notation that at the moment, there are no
deliveries in the street in question. The suspected reason is typhoid
fever. Well, one does not know. Money is not being returned, but no
receipts arrive, either. On November 12, a transport went to Minsk.
A few people supposedly smuggled some letters home by way of the
army post office, though I never actually saw any such letters. It's the
same story for the people who went to Riga on November 27 and in
January. I do, however, know one lady here who really did read such
a letter. Of the thousand people who went to Riga on November 17,
not one ever wrote a line. Thus the widespread rumor started that they
were shot on the way, or were murdered in some other fashion. Obviously, all these things do not increase the courage of those who are*

[2] The Nazi's new name for Lodz in Poland.

affected by the evacuation. Thus there is a vast increase in the number
of suicides. . . .

Hermann Samter, letter of January 26,
1942; Gerhard Schönberner, ed., *Wir
haben es gesehen* (Hamburg, 1962), pp.
296–97.

VON DER EINSATZGRUPPE A DURCHGEFÜHRTE
JUDENEXEKUTIONEN
(Jewish Executions Undertaken by Special Squad A)

PETERSBURG

KRASNOGWARDEISK

REVAL

963

DAGO

JUDENFREI
(Free of Jews)

3600

ÖSEL
ARENSBURG

RIGAER
BUCHT

RIGA

GHETTO 2500

35238

GHETTO 4500
SCHAULEN

DUNABURG

GHETTO 950

136421

KAUEN
GHETTO 15000

41828

MINSK

GESCHÄTZTE ZAHL DER NOCH VORHANDENEN JUDEN 128000
(Estimated number of remaining Jews: 128,000)

(Baltic Sea)
OSTSEE

. . . When I arrived, there were about 25,000 Jews in the district of Slonim. Of that number, about 16,000 were in the city of Slonim, so that more than two thirds of the city's population were Jews. To construct a ghetto was impossible, since I had neither barbed wire nor the necessary guards. I therefore, from the very beginning, made my preparations for a major Action. Expropriation was the first step, and the furniture and supplies that became available were used to equip all German offices here, those of the armed forces included. We generously aided other districts, too, so that given the growth of all departments, there are shortages in my own offices now. Stuff that was not fit for Germans was released to the city to be sold to the populace, with the proceeds being added to our official revenues. There followed an exact survey of the Jews according to number, age, and profession, and the segregation of all craftsmen and skilled workers and their being marked by special identifications and separate housing. The Action undertaken by the Secret Police on November 13 freed me from all useless eaters, and the approximately 7000 Jews who now remain in the city of Slonim all are a part of the labor force. Their permanent fear of death makes them willing workers, and in the spring, they will be examined and sorted out with a view to a further reduction. . . .

> Report of District Commissioner Gert Erren, January 25, 1941; Schönberner, *Wir haben es gesehen*, pp. 133–34.

. . . On May 11, another transport of Jews (1000 pieces) arrived in Minsk from Vienna, and was taken from the station directly to the above-mentioned ditch. . . .

> Report of SS sergeant [signature illegible], May 17, 1942; *Unsere Ehre heisst Treue* (Vienna, 1965), p. 236.

## "THE JEWS ARE TO BLAME": THE PUBLIC LINE

The shootings took place beyond Germany's borders, and not a single news item concerning them was allowed to find its way into print. Still, certain rumors did circulate, and besides, discriminatory devices such as the Jewish star were meant to be visible. Consequently, not long after the star had been introduced, Joseph Goebbels wrote a long editorial, justifying the anti-Semitic measures, in *Das Reich*, the Nazis' prestige weekly. His article is followed by some private comments Hitler made half a year later.

# The Jews Are To Blame!

## By Reich Minister Dr. Goebbels

World Jewry's historic guilt for the outbreak and extension of this war has been so abundantly proven that no additional words need to be lost over the matter. The Jews wanted their war. Now they have it. But what is also coming true for them is the Führer's prophecy which he voiced in his Reichstag speech of January 30, 1939. It was that if international financial Jewry succeeded in plunging the nations into another world war, the result would not be the Bolshevization of the world and thus the victory of Jewry, but the destruction of the Jewish race in Europe.

We now are witnessing the acid test of this prophecy, and thus Jewry is experiencing a fate which is hard but more than deserved. Pity or even regrets are entirely out of place here. World Jewry, in starting this war, made an entirely wrong estimate of the forces at its disposal, and is now suffering the same gradual process of destruction which it had planned for us, and which it would apply without hesitation were it to possess the power to do so. It is in line with their own law, "An eye for an eye, a tooth for a tooth," that the ruin of the Jews is now taking place.

In this historic conflict every Jew is our enemy, no matter whether he is vegetating in a Polish ghetto, or still supporting his parasitical existence in Berlin or Hamburg, or blowing the war trumpet in New York or Washington. By reason of their birth and race, all Jews are members of an international conspiracy against National Socialist Germany. They wish for its defeat and destruction, and do whatever is in their power to help bring it about. That in Germany itself, the means at their disposal toward this end are small, certainly is not due to their being loyal here, but solely to the fact that we took those measures against them which we judged to be proper.

One of those measures is the introduction of the Jew's star, which every Jew is obliged to wear visibly. This is designed to mark him externally, too, above all so that if he should make the least attempt to injure the German national community, he can immediately be recognized as a Jew. It is an extraordinarily humane order, a prophylactic health measure, as it were, designed to keep the Jew from creeping into our ranks, unrecognized, to sow disunion among us.

When the Jews, a few weeks ago, appeared in the streets of Berlin adorned with their Jew's stars, the first impression among the capital's citizens was one of general amazement. Only a very small number among us knew that there were still so many Jews in Berlin. Everyone discovered, in his district or his neighborhood, some fellow who acted as though he could not harm a fly, who had, it was true, attracted some occasional attention by his griping and complaining, but whom no one would have suspected of being a Jew. Who among us, please, had any idea that the enemy was standing right next to him, that he was a silent, or a cleverly prompting, listener to conversations in the street, in the subway, or in the line that was forming in front of the tobacco shop? There are Jews who can hardly be told apart any more by their looks. As much as they could, they have assimilated themselves in this respect too. They are the most dangerous ones. It is symptomatic that any measure we take against the Jews is reported the very next day in the British and American press. The Jews, then, even now have their secret lines of communication to the enemy nations, and use them not only in their own cause, but in all matters that are militarily vital to the Reich. Thus the enemy is right in our midst. What, therefore, is more obvious than to make him at least externally recognizable to every citizen?

. . . How sad, compared with this international problem which has bothered mankind for millennia, are the stupid, sentimentally thoughtless arguments of some still extant pals of the Jews! How their eyes, noses, and mouths would fly open if they ever saw their dear Jews in the possession of power. But then it would be too late. And therefore it is the duty of a national leadership to make sure, by the means it deems proper, that this will never come to pass. There is a difference between humans and humans, just as there is a difference between animals and animals. We know good and bad humans, just as we know good and bad animals. The fact that the Jew still lives among us is no proof that he is one of us, no more than the flea's domestic residence makes him a domestic animal. If Herr Bramsig or Frau Knöterich feel a touch of pity as they look upon an old woman wearing a Jew's star, let them remember please that a distant cousin of this old lady, Nathan Kaufman by name, is sitting in New York and has prepared a plan according to which all Germans under 60 would be sterilized. Let them remember that the son of her distant uncle is a warmonger by the name of Baruch or Morgenthau or Untermayer, who is standing behind Mr. Roosevelt, urging him to go to war, and if he should succeed in that aim, some decent but ignorant American soldier might shoot Herr Bramsig's or Frau Knöterich's son quite dead —all to the greater glory of Jewry, of which this old woman is a part, too, no matter how fragile or pity-inspiring she might act. . . .

So, superfluous though it might be, let me say once more:

1. The Jews are our destruction. They provoked and brought about this war. What they mean to achieve by it is to destroy the German state and nation. This plan must be frustrated.

2. There is no difference between Jew and Jew. Every Jew is a sworn enemy of the German people. If he fails to display his hostility against us, it is merely out of cowardice and slyness, but not because his heart is free of it.

3. Every German soldier's death in this war is the Jews' responsibility. They have it on their conscience; hence they must pay for it.

4. Anyone wearing the Jew's star has been marked as an enemy of the nation. Any person who still maintains social relations with him is one of them, and must be considered a Jew himself and treated as such. He deserves the contempt of the entire nation, which he has deserted in its gravest hour to join the side of those who hate it.

5. The Jews enjoy the protection of the enemy nations. No further proof is needed of their destructive role among our people.

6. The Jews are the messengers of the enemy in our midst. Anyone joining them is going over to the enemy in time of war.

7. The Jews have no claim to pretend to have rights equal to ours. Wherever they want to open their mouths, in the streets, in the lines in front of the stores, or on public transportation, they are to be silenced. They are to be silenced not only because they are wrong on principle, but because they are Jews and have no voice in the community.

8. If Jews pull a sentimental act for you, bear in mind that they are speculating on your forgetfulness. Show them immediately that you see right through them and punish them with contempt.

9. A decent enemy, after his defeat, deserves our generosity. But the Jew is no decent enemy. He only pretends to be one.

10. **The Jews are to blame for this war. The treatment we give them does them no wrong. They have more than deserved it. . . .**

Joseph Goebbels, "Die Juden sind schuld!"
*Das Reich,* November 16, 1941; in Hans
Dieter Müller, *Facsimile Querschnitt durch
Das Reich* (Munich, 1964), pp. 98–101.

*May 15, 1942, noon*

. . . *It was for the very same Jew who stabbed us in the back that
our so-called bourgeoisie was lamenting as he was being moved to the
East. What was so remarkable about this was that the same bourgeoisie
could not have cared less when 250,000 or 300,000 German men and
women a year emigrated from Germany, and about 75 per cent of the
German emigrants to Australia died on the journey over.*[3] . . .

*No one who was shedding his crocodile's tears for a Jew transported
to the East considered the fact that the Jew, being a parasite, was the
most weather-proof of humans on this earth, and in contrast to a
German could survive in Lapland as much as in the tropics. Of course,
these philistine folk usually were people who were ever so proud of
knowing their bible, but who even so did not recall that according to
the reports of the Old Testament, the Jews had come to harm neither
by a stay in the desert nor by a march through the Red Sea. . . .*

Picker, *Hitlers Tischgespräche,* p. 348.

## EXTERMINATION: THE GASSINGS

At the time that Hitler was talking, a new murder method had
already been decided upon. Early in May 1942, the first extermination
camp employing gas began operating in Poland. (Previously only mobile
gas vans had been used, largely on an experimental basis.) There followed the establishment of several other such camps, the largest of
which was at Auschwitz. The camps operated until fall of 1944, when
by Himmler's order, exterminations were stopped. All of the camps
were located in Nazi-occupied Poland rather than in Germany itself;
this was one of the lessons learned from the euthanasia program. They
were run, like the entire system of the concentration camps, by the SS,
and employed many of the people who had learned their trade in
*Aktion T 4.*

Other means of extermination continued to be used as well—mass

---

[3] The figures are imaginary.

shootings, labor to the point of collapse, starvation, withholding of medical care and drugs, torture. But considering the number of victims involved, and the occasional emotional difficulties encountered by the executioners, who might balk at shooting children, for instance, gassing proved by far the most efficient method.

In 1943, Hans Frank, the Nazi Governor-general of Poland, made a rough estimate of the number killed in his territory. Three years and a lost war later, in the spring of 1946 at Nuremberg, the commandant of Auschwitz gave the figures on the number killed in his camp alone. In the fall of the same year, while awaiting execution of the death sentence passed on him by the Poles, he corrected these figures, which on reflection struck him as exaggerated.

> . . . *Things are very clear here. To somebody who says, What's to become of the National Socialist party? we can reply, The National Socialist party surely will survive the Jews. We started with three and a half million Jews here. Of that number, only a few work companies remain. Everybody else has—let us say—emigrated.*
>
> Hans Frank, August 2, 1943; Piotrowski, *Dziennik Hansa Franka*, p. 362.

> *I, RUDOLF FRANZ FERDINAND HOESS, being first duly sworn, depose and say as follows:*
>
> *1. I am forty-six years old, and have been a member of the NSDAP since 1922; a member of the SS since 1934; a member of the Waffen-SS since 1939. I was a member from 1 December 1934 of the SS Guard Unit, the so-called Deathshead Formation (Totenkopf Verband).*
>
> *2. I have been constantly associated with the administration of concentration camps since 1934, serving at Dachau until 1938; then as Adjutant in Sachsenhausen from 1938 to May 1, 1940, when I was appointed Commandant of Auschwitz. I commanded Auschwitz until 1 December, 1943, and estimate that at least 2,500,000 victims were executed and exterminated there by gassing and burning, and at least another half million succumbed to starvation and disease, making a total dead of about 3,000,000. This figure represents about 70% or 80% of all persons sent to Auschwitz. . . .*
>
> I.M.T., Document 3868-PS, XXXIII, 275–76.

> . . . *During previous interrogations, I put the number of Jews who were sent to Auschwitz for extermination at 2½ million. This figure was supplied by Eichmann, who gave it to my superior officer, SS General Glücks, when he was ordered to report to the Reich Leader of the SS shortly before Berlin was encircled. . . . I think the number of 2½*

million is much too high. Even in Auschwitz, there were limits to the
possibilities of destruction. . . .
   The two great crematories I and II were built in the winter of
1942–1943, and put into use in the spring of 1943. Each had five
three-retort ovens, and each could cremate about 2000 bodies within
24 hours. Technical reasons connected with keeping the fires going
made it impossible to increase the capacity of the ovens. Attempts to
do so resulted in serious damage, which on several occasions meant a
complete breakdown of operations. . . .

Rudolf Höss, Kommandant in Auschwitz
(Stuttgart, 1958), pp. 162–63 and 160.

## "A PAGE OF GLORY . . ."

   Quite possibly, Höss's later qualifications were justified. The number
of people murdered at Auschwitz may have been closer to two million.
And in general, the total figure of 6 million Jewish victims that has
often been mentioned is very likely wrong, and that of only approximately 5 million more nearly correct.
   There is, however, no argument about the pride the Nazis took in
their achievement. In 1943, Himmler addressed these words to an
assembly of ranking SS leaders in Posen:

   . . . Let me, in all frankness, mention a terribly hard chapter to
you. Among ourselves, we can openly talk about it, though we will
never speak a word of it in public. . . . I am speaking about the evacuation of the Jews, the extermination of the Jewish people. That is
one of those things where the words come so easily. "The Jewish people
will be exterminated," says every party member, "of course. It's in our
program. Exclusion of the Jews, extermination. We'll take care of it."
And then they come, these nice 80 million Germans, and every one
of them has his decent Jew. Sure, the others are swine, but this one is
a fine Jew. Of all those who talk like that, not one has been a witness,
not one has stood his ground. Most of you will know what it means
to have seen 100 corpses together, or 500, or 1000. To have made one's
way through that, and—some instances of human weakness aside—
to have remained a decent person throughout, that is what has made us
hard. That is a page of glory in our history that never has been and
never will be written. . . .
   The riches they had, we took away from them. I gave strict orders,
which were executed by SS General Pohl, that these riches, down to
the last penny, were of course to go to the State. We ourselves took

nothing. *Individuals who acted counter to this will be punished in accordance with an order I gave in the beginning, and in which I made the threat that he who took but a single mark would face death. A number of SS men, not many, sinned against this, and death will be their share, and without mercy. We had the moral right, and the duty, toward our nation to kill this people which wished to kill us. But we do not have the right to enrich ourselves with a single fur or a watch, a mark, a cigarette, or who knows what else. We do not, because we were exterminating a bacillus, wish to be infected by that bacillus in the end and die. I will not sit idly by as even the smallest of putrid spots appears or remains. Where such a spot should appear, we together will cauterize it. But in all, we can say that we fulfilled this heaviest of tasks in love to our people. And we suffered no harm in our essence, in our soul, in our character. . . .*

Heinrich Himmler, October 4, 1943, I.M.T., Document 1919-PS, XXIX, 145–46.

# 11

## RESISTANCE

*Now the whole world will assail and curse us. But I am as solidly convinced as ever I was that what we did was right. I believe that Hitler is the archenemy not only of Germany, but of the whole world. When a few hours from now, I shall stand before God's judgment seat, to offer an account of what I have done and what I have failed to do, I think my conscience will be clear as I defend my actions in the fight against Hitler. As God once promised Abraham that he would not destroy Sodom if but ten just men could be found there, so I hope that God, for our sakes, will not destroy Germany. None of us can complain about his death. He who entered our circle donned the shirt of Nessus. The moral worth of a man only begins at the point where he is ready to sacrifice his life for his convictions.*

> General Henning von Tresckow, be-
> fore his suicide at the Russian front,
> July 21, 1944.

## "NOT MY KIND OF GERMANISM": A RESIGNATION FROM THE ACADEMY

From the very beginning, there were Germans who, despite the re-gime's external successes, despite the propaganda and the secret police, resisted National Socialism. Their resistance took many forms, from quiet noncooperation to active plans for revolt. Among those who long before the mass murders began sensed the regime's true nature, and drew the personal consequences, was Ricarda Huch (1864–1947), a distinguished novelist and popular historian. In the spring of 1933, as

writers politically left of center such as Heinrich Mann, or racially
undesirable such as Alfred Döblin, were being expelled from the Prussian
Academy of Arts and Sciences in pursuit of "alignment," she decided
to resign from the Academy in protest. In a letter to the Academy's
President, the composer Max von Schillings (not precisely a rabid
National Socialist himself), she explained her decision:

Heidelberg, April 9, 1933

Dear President von Schillings:
Let me first thank you for the warm interest you have taken in having
me remain in the Academy. I would very much like you to understand
why I cannot follow your wish. That a German's feelings are German
I would consider to be just about self-evident, but the definition of
what is German, and what acting in a German manner means—those
are things where opinions differ. What the present government pre-
scribes by way of patriotic convictions is not my kind of Germanism.
The centralization, the use of compulsion, the brutal methods, the
defamation of those who hold different convictions, the boastful self-
praise—these are matters which I consider un-German and disastrous.
As I consider the divergence between this opinion of mine and that
being ordered by the state, I find it impossible to remain in an Academy
that is a part of the state. You say that the declaration submitted to me
by the Academy would not prevent me from the free expression of my
opinions. But "loyal cooperation, in the spirit of the changed historical
situation, on matters affecting national and cultural tasks that fall
within the jurisdiction of the Academy" requires an agreement with the
government's program which in my case does not exist. Besides, I
would find no newspaper or magazine that would print an opposition
opinion. Thus the right to the free expression of opinion would remain
quite theoretical.
You mention Herr Heinrich Mann and Dr. Döblin. It is true that
Herr Heinrich Mann and I have disagreed with each other. Nor have I
always agreed with Herr Döblin, though on some things I did. But at
any rate, I would wish that all non-Jewish Germans were seeking, as
conscientiously as he has, to know and to do what is right, to be as
frank and honest and decent as I have always found him to be. In my
view, the anti-Jewish rabble-rousing left him no choice but to act as
he has. That my departure from the Academy is no demonstration of
sympathy for the gentlemen involved, despite the special respect and
sympathy I feel for Dr. Döblin, anyone who knows me or my books
will realize.
I hereby resign from the Academy.

s. RICARDA HUCH

Marie Baum, *Leuchtende Spur, Das Leben
Ricarda Huchs* (Fourth edition, Tübingen,
1964), pp. 343–45.

# "KLEIST WOULD NOT REMAIN ALIVE FOR LONG": A POET IS DISILLUSIONED

Another German writer who came to recognize the regime for what it was, was Gottfried Benn. Benn (1886–1956), a Berlin physician and one of Germany's most prominent modern poets, originally had been a defender of the new government, pleading its cause in 1933 against the attacks of a number of émigré writers. Disillusionment came quickly. In 1936, he wrote to a friend and critic:

. . . Where is it going to end? Furtwängler no longer conducts.[1] Hindemith is in Ankara.[2] Poelzig is going there.[3] A book about Barlach was banned.[4] I am publicly called a little pig. A Corinth[5] exhibit in Basel is so successful that it provokes the hatred, the ineradicable hatred, of these people, because Corinth is one of "those" artists. Or you might say more simply because he is an artist. One man is being attacked for being Alpine, another for being Mediterranean, a third for being a humanist, a fourth for being a Christian. They fight everyone; the only thing they cannot do is to produce something themselves. Pull out, kill, keep down, that is the side of eugenics they are masters at. But the other side, to have some feeling for what creativity is, to lead it, to broaden its scope, to direct things in silence, of that they have no idea. It's not heroic enough, it's too unNordic. . . .
The other day, I wondered what would happen if Penthesilea[6] were to be published today. A play about a woman who loves a man, Achilles, kills him, and tears him apart with her teeth. Tears him apart! What are we, dogs, no we are Teutons! Perverted nobleman dares offer his animal lust to an audience of Teutonic ladies! Degenerate cast of offi-

[1] Wilhelm Furtwängler (1886–1954) was in temporary retirement following a notable exchange of letters with Goebbels in 1933, in which he had told the propaganda minister that he could see no difference between Jewish and Aryan but only between "good and bad art."
[2] Paul Hindemith (1895–1963), at first praised for the supposedly Nordic qualities of his work, became one of the favorite targets of Nazi criticism against "culturally Bolshevik" modern music. He moved to the United States in 1940.
[3] Hans Poelzig (1869–1936), whose Broadcasting House was something of a Berlin landmark, had aroused Nazi ire by his modern approach to architecture.
[4] Ernst Barlach (1870–1938), sculptor, painter, and poet, not unlike Hindemith, went from being appreciated for the "Nordic" character of his work to being ostracized as one of the principal exponents of what the Nazis grouped as "degenerate" art.
[5] Louis Corinth (1858–1925), German postimpressionist painter.
[6] The play by Heinrich von Kleist (1777–1811), member of an old and very distinguished aristocratic family, and Prussia's greatest dramatic poet.

cers and squires sullies chaste German heroic women with his filthy
orgasms! Etc. In short, Kleist would not remain alive for long.

I do not write you all this because of my personal resentment against
the stupid Schw[arze] K[orps],[7] no, I write because I am sad. I am sure
that one cannot ruin Germany intellectually, but some deep wounds
are being inflicted. It is being robbed of much. Because of a theory,
which is very German again, because of the Nordic theory. For which
there is no evidence but only hopes, and hopes which I think are misguided. I'd gladly let myself be converted, but I can see no starting
point for such a conversion. I see that everything that still exists dates
from an earlier age. It is what Goethe nourished, what Schiller glowed
for, what Herder and Humboldt discovered and extended, and what
Nietzsche put into final form and transmitted to the new century. This
German education still supports everything. It is this German depth
which has kept the present flatness and impertinence from turning into
catastrophe. This inspired stream of an intermingled Europe, land between the rivers, heir to unresolved tensions, of incredible wealth in
talent and dreams—this is what still surrounds, night and day, these
rudiments, these mandrake roots, who fancy themselves a new species
and a new beginning. . . .

Gottfried Benn to Frank Maraun, May 11,
1936; Gottfried Benn, *Ausgewählte Briefe*
(Second edition, Wiesbaden, 1959), pp.
70–72.

## A SPEECH TO GERMAN YOUTH

The consequence that Benn, as well as some others, drew from their
convictions was "inner emigration." Unlike Thomas Mann, for instance,
whose emigration was very much outward, Benn remained in Germany,
avoiding all contemporary themes in his published writings, but engaging
in no open polemics with the regime either. It was a relatively safe
course to take, particularly since Benn chose what struck him as the
most aristocratic form of inner emigration, which was to rejoin the
army. But there were other forms of resistance to the total state that,
in the event, were not substantially more dangerous. In the early years
in particular, there were a good many things an individual could do
without automatically finding himself in prison, provided always that
he observed two rules. One was to avoid the public forum; the other

[7] The weekly of the SS had attacked Benn for his modernism.

was to refrain from organizing clandestine resistance groups. Thus, the German ambassador to United States resigned as soon as Hitler became Chancellor. He believed in democratic government, he told his foreign minister, and had no desire to serve the new regime. He was retired on his full legal pension, and left unmolested by the police. Thus a Bavarian district attorney, when he learned about the tortures practiced in the concentration camp in his area, started a judicial investigation of the crimes being committed by the guards. An abrupt end was ordered to the investigation, but nothing happened to the district attorney.

It helped, of course, to be a person of some prominence. The ambassador's name was von Prittwitz und Gaffron. Ricarda Huch was much too famous to be summarily arrested. A district attorney was a man of consequence in a society where the civil service ranked very high. But others, too, could withhold cooperation without in all cases facing the direst of consequences. Thus, the worst that would normally happen to an SS man whose conscience rebelled at a shooting order was expulsion from the SS.

Public protests, however, were a different matter. Here, there was no tolerance. Here, too, the regime's control of the media made it next to impossible to reach any sizeable audience. One of the very few who found both the courage and an audience was the novelist Ernst Wiechert (1887–1950), a man who politically came from the Conservative right. Avoiding any direct mention of National Socialism, he addressed these words to a large student group in Munich in 1935:

> . . . It probably is the fate of every revolution that those who march in and alter it pervert the meaning of renewal. That they not only abolish the monarchy but want the king's severed head as well, that they do away not only with the clergy but with God as well. That they believe that every fifth grader must wrap his fist around a German oak and "do something." They do not know about the eternal features of a nation's history which cannot be changed by lesser hands. They do not know that a stream of blood which is millennia old cannot be diverted into another riverbed by slogans. They do not know how quietly the truly heroic walks upon this earth, although all they would have to do is to look into the face of a nation which for 20 years now has acted with quiet heroism. And they have long forgotten how calmly and devoutly and humbly Pestalozzi taught his children. Oh yes, it may happen that a nation stops distinguishing between right and wrong, and that it will consider every one of its battles to be "right." But this nation already stands on a steep incline, and the law of its fall is already written. It may well be that this nation will still win a gladiator's fame, and in its battles construct an ethic that we might call a prizefighter's ethic. But

*the scales have been raised over this nation, and on every wall the hand
will appear and write in letters of fire.* . . .

Ernst Wiechert, *Der Dichter und die Zeit;
Rede, gehalten am 16. April 1935 im Audi-
torium Maximum der Universität München*
(Zurich, 1945), pp. 25–27.

# "THE COMING WAR . . .":
# A WARNING FROM ABROAD

Even Wiechert's speech did not result in his immediate arrest,
although in 1938, he spent two months in Buchenwald concentration
camp for his active support of the Confessing Church. The next offense,
Dr. Goebbels told him privately, would lead to his "physical destruction." What opposition appeals there still were now were largely clandestine ones, or came from abroad. The most celebrated one among
the latter was the reply that Thomas Mann sent to the University of
Bonn in 1937, after being told that he had been deprived of his honorary
degree. His letter contains a number of forecasts and judgments that
events showed to be very much in error—Germany, he said for instance,
was on the verge of bankruptcy, and would never find a single ally in
the event of another war. But the core of his indictment was all too
true:

> . . . *The sole possible aim and purpose of the National Socialist
> system can only be this: to prepare the German people for the "coming
> war" by the ruthless elimination, suppression, and extermination of any
> sort of sentiment opposing such a war, to make the German people into
> an utterly obedient, uncritical instrument of war, blind and fanatic in
> its ignorance. The system can have no other aim and purpose, no other
> excuse. All the sacrifices of freedom, justice, human happiness, all the
> secret and open crimes which it has so blithely committed, can be
> justified only by the aim of making the nation unconditionally fit for
> war. Were the idea of war to be removed, of war as an aim in itself, the
> system would be nothing but the sheerest exploitation—it would have
> neither meaning nor function.* . . .

Thomas Mann to the Dean of the University of Bonn, January 1, 1937; Erika Mann,
ed., *Thomas Mann, Briefe 1937–1947*
(Frankfurt, 1963), p. 13.

# BEYOND OBEDIENCE:
# A MILITARY WARNING

Actually, some of the strongest warnings against the coming war came from the German military itself. The army's commander-in-chief counseled caution to Hitler. (He would, before long, be dismissed in disgrace.) The chief of the army general staff, when he realized that Hitler's war plans were unalterable, resigned in protest in 1938, and began active plans for the overthrow of the regime. (He would commit suicide when the plans failed.) Shortly before his resignation, his counterpart in the navy, chief of naval staff Vice-Admiral Guse, wrote the memorandum whose central passage is printed below. Its presumable recipient was the navy's commander-in-chief. Guse's language was moderate, and the arguments he used were pragmatic rather than moral—there was no other conceivable hope of reaching Hitler—yet the gist of what he was saying was perfectly plain and it required a good deal of courage to say it.

. . . I believe that the Führer should still be able to sway the course of events, and that he truly holds the fate of Europe in his hands. If at this moment (by a peace speech to the Reichstag, for instance) he should give to the world the clear proof of his desire for peace, there is hope for a general relaxation of tension. There can be no doubt that in a conflict European in scope Germany would be the loser, and that the Führer's whole work so far would be in jeopardy. So far, I have not spoken to any ranking officer in any of the three branches of the armed services who did not share this opinion, or who did not fear that considering the political tension of the moment, an attack on the Czech state would develop into a European war. In this situation, the responsible advisers of the Führer have not only the duty of obedience to his orders. They also have the duty to do all that is in their power, and that includes taking every necessary logical step, to see to it that a development which threatens the continued existence of the nation is stopped in time. . . .

July 17, 1938; *Die Vollmacht des Gewissens* (Munich, 1956), p. 312.

## A QUESTION OF NUMBERS:
## HOW MANY RESISTERS?

The question of how many people showed themselves immune to both the blandishments and the threats of National Socialism is impossible to answer with absolute certitude. Estimates of how many Germans, from Communists to Conservatives, spent some time either in prison or in a concentration camp for political reasons during the Nazi period vary between half a million and one million. Himmler, in his speech to the gauleiters of August 1944, asked his listeners to consider the folly of the anti-Hitler conspirators of July 20; they had meant to release all concentration camp inmates, he said, when "we have 550,000 prisoners, of whom about 100,000 are foreigners." The military statistics, which are precise on numbers, though less precise on the reasons for each verdict, show that between August 1939 and January 1945, 24,559 members of the German armed forces were sentenced to death.

As it was, the war both narrowed and broadened the resistance movement's potential. It narrowed it, since it made nation and government identical to some previous doubters, who now felt that resistance might too easily blend into treason. Besides, the early victories of German arms brought tremendous prestige to Hitler. On the other hand, as Hitler's luck turned, after Stalingrad and the German reverses that followed it, the number of people who were having some second thoughts grew.

The following excerpt is from a secret memorandum intended for the use of top government and party officials. It is one of a series of such memoranda, put out biweekly by the domestic intelligence division of the Secret Police, and based on the reports of several thousand agents in various parts of Germany. It deals with the public mood following Goebbels's total war speech of February 1943 (quoted on pp. 91–92 above), and goes on to say:

> . . . According to information from western Germany, but from other parts of the nation as well, there is a good deal of talk to the effect that the enemy air offensive is a consequence of the proclamation of total war. For what many people understand by the term total war is not so much the total application of all energies to the production of armaments, but the transition to the total use of every available means, without restrictions, in fighting the enemy. Many people therefore felt the proclamation of total war to be a challenge to which the enemy

could not but respond. This misunderstanding led to a certain animosity against the capital, from which the proclamation of total war was made. This attitude is being characterized by a rhyme which supposedly has a wide circulation in the industrial area:

> Keep on flying, Tommy dear
> All of us are miners here
> Fly on to Berlin, we say
> That's where they all shouted "Yea."

SD report of May 6, 1943; Heinz Boberach, ed., *Meldungen aus dem Reich, Auswahl aus den geheimen Lageberichten des Sicherheitsdienstes der SS* (Neuwied, 1965), p. 390.

## "AGAINST THE SPIRIT OF FORCE, ARROGANCE, INTOLERANCE": A FARMER'S SON AND A MARSHAL'S DESCENDANT

It was one thing to repeat irreverent verse, or to tell a joke involving Göring's obesity or Goebbels's mendacity. To do so might land a man in a great deal of trouble, but it hardly endangered the survival of the state. It was something else again to oppose, at the conscious risk of one's life, the very essence of what the state stood for. "The moral worth of a man only begins at the point where he is ready to sacrifice his life for his convictions. . . ." This was too Prussian, too Kantian, a sentiment for most, but there follow excerpts from the last letters of two men among many who did pay for their convictions with their deaths. One is from a farmer's son from the Sudeten area, and incidentally shows that there were exceptions to the rule that SS orders could be contravened with impunity by the racially pure. The other is from Count Helmuth James von Moltke, the eldest son of a great-nephew of the Field Marshal of the Bismarckian era. Opponents of the regime of all shades of political opinion had met at his estate to discuss plans for a post-Hitler Germany. He was arrested in 1944, and tried and executed a year later. (Resisters could be found among all German groups and classes, but there is, among the most active of them, a certain preponderance of Prussian names: Moltke, Tresckow, Schlabrendorff, Bussche, Trott zu Solz, Lehndorff, Yorck von Wartenburg, Kleist, and two von der Schulenburgs.)

*February 3, 1944*

*Dear Parents:*

*I must tell you the sad news that I have been sentenced to death, I and Gustav G. We would not let the SS have our signatures, so they sentenced us to death. You'll recall writing me not to join the SS, my comrade Gustav G. did not sign either. We both would rather die than stain our consciences with such atrocities. I know what the SS has to do. Oh, my dear parents, no matter how hard it is for me and you, forgive me everything. If I should have hurt you, please forgive me and pray for me.*

*Suppose I were to die in the war and had a guilty conscience, that would be sad for you too. Many parents are still going to lose their children. Many SS men die too. I thank you for all the kindnesses you have shown me since my childhood. Forgive me, pray for me. . . .*

> Helmut Gollwitzer, Käthe Kuhn, and Reinhold Schneider, eds., *Du hast mich heimgesucht bei Nacht* (Third edition, Munich, 1962), p. 233.

*. . . All my life, even in school, I fought against a spirit of narrowness and force, of arrogance, intolerance, and pitiless, absolute logic which is a part of the German equipment, and which found its embodiment in the National Socialist state. And I did what I could. to help vanquish this spirit, with its terrible consequences such as excessive nationalism, racial persecution, irreligion, materialism. . . .*

> Count Moltke to his sons, January 1945, Helmuth James Graf von Moltke, *Letzte Briefe aus dem Gefängnis Tegel* (Berlin, 1963), p. 9.

## WHITE ROSE

Moltke and his friends had largely eschewed violence. The regime, they felt, would have to prove its utter bankruptcy to every last German by the resounding loss of the war. Besides, as long as the Nazis controlled both the machinery of the state and the public communications media, it was an illusion to think in terms of revolution. Hence, they tended to be more concerned with ideas for a postwar Germany than with anti-Hitler plots. (This did not mean complete passivity, but what action they took tended to be restricted to saving individuals who were in danger.)

Among the few groups that disagreed with this attitude strongly enough to engage in plans for open rebellion was one led by two Munich students, Hans Scholl and his sister Sophie. Hans Scholl was born in 1918, and his reservations about the Nazis went back to his Hitler Youth days. He became active in the resistance after his return from the Russian front in 1942. Together with his sister and a number of other fellow students, he organized, under the name of the White Rose, a number of underground resistance cells in Munich, Freiburg, and Berlin.

His boldest act also was his last. On February 18, 1943, he dropped a large quantity of leaflets down a lightshaft into the courtyard of Munich University. He was discovered and arrested. So were many of his friends, including the pamphlet's principal author, Kurt Huber, Professor of Philosophy at Munich. All were tried, sentenced to death, and executed, Hans and Sophie Scholl within four days of their arrest, on February 22, 1943. A surviving sister, Inge Scholl, has recorded his last words. "And Hans, when he put his head upon the block, called out, in a voice loud enough to be heard throughout the large prison: 'Long live freedom.'"

This was the text of the pamphlet he had distributed that February 18, 1943.

*Fellow students:*
. . . The day of reckoning has come, the day when German youth will settle accounts with the vilest tyranny ever endured by our nation. In the name of German youth, we demand from Adolf Hitler's state the restoration of personal freedom, a German's most precious possession, which it took from us by base deceit.

We grew up in a state where every free expression of opinion has been ruthlessly suppressed. Hitler Youth, storm troops, and SS have tried, in the most receptive years of our lives, to regiment, to revolutionize, and to narcotize us. "Ideological education" was the name for this despicable method of suffocating budding independent thought in a fog of empty phrases. A selected group of leaders (and it is impossible to imagine a group more devious and at the same time more bigoted) is training future Nazi bosses in party castles, to be exploiters and killers without God, without shame, without conscience, to give blind and unreasoning obedience to those above them. . . .

There can be but one word of action for us: Fight the party! Quit the party organizations, where all discussion in still being stifled. Leave the classrooms of the SS leaders high and low, and of the party sycophants. What is at stake is true science and genuine intellectual freedom. No threats can frighten us, not even that of closing our universities. Each of us must join in the fight for our future, for a life in freedom and honor in a state that is aware of its moral obligations.

Freedom and honor! For ten long years, Hitler and his accomplices have worn out, abused, and corrupted these words to the point of disgust, as only dilettantes could, who threw the nation's highest values to the swine. What freedom and honor mean to them they have shown in ten years of destroying all actual and spiritual freedom, of destroying the moral substance of the German nation. The eyes of even the most dull-witted German have been opened by the frightful bloodbath they arranged, and are still arranging every day, over all of Europe for the sake of what to them is the freedom and honor of the German nation. The German name will be forever disgraced unless Germany's youth finally rises, avenges and atones at the same time, crushes its tormentors, and builds a new concept of Europe. Students! The eyes of the German nation are upon us. Germany expects from us, from the might of the spirit, the destruction of the National Socialist terror in 1943, as it expected the destruction of the Napoleonic terror in 1813. The flames of the Berezina and of Stalingrad signal to us, the dead of Stalingrad implore us:

"Act, then, my nation, see the beacons' blaze!" [8]

Our nation shall rise against the enslavement of Europe by National Socialism in a new, true burst of freedom and honor.

> Inge Scholl, *Die weisse Rose* (Frankfurt, 1964), pp. 151–55.

## JULY 20, 1944

Moltke had been right. Appeals to open rebellion were brave but doomed. Hitler was not Bonaparte. 1943 was not 1813. Nor, for that matter, had there ever been a rising against Napoleon in his own country.

There did, however, remain one slender hope, one alternative to letting Hitler take Germany to utter ruin. It was a coup d'état from above—assassinate Hitler, and follow this by seizing the government with the aid of sympathizers close to the machinery of power, especially in the army. The principal leaders in this plot were Carl Goerdeler (1884–1944), Ludwig Beck (1880–1944), and Count Claus von Stauffenberg (1907–1944). Goerdeler was a former Lord Mayor of Leipzig, who had resigned his office in 1936 when the local party leader removed the monument to Felix Mendelssohn-Bartholdy from in front of Leipzig's concert hall. General Beck was the former chief of the general staff, who had left that post when he realized how absolutely committed

---

[8] This is the opening line of Theodor Körner's 1813 poem "Appeal," calling on the Germans to rise against Napoleon's rule—"Make way for freedom, cleanse this earth, this German land of ours, with your blood!"

Hitler was to war. Colonel von Stauffenberg was a disabled and much decorated veteran of the African and Russian campaigns, with an abiding hate for Hitler and his works.

The story of their attempt, and failure, is well-known—how Stauffenberg, following several earlier abortive efforts to kill Hitler, left a briefcase containing a time bomb in the Führer's headquarters on July 20, 1944, how the bomb went off but failed to kill Hitler, how after the conspirators' brief seizure of the war ministry in Berlin, their coup ended in disaster. What has received somewhat less attention, however, are the amount of planning behind the conspiracy, and the motives of the plotters. Something of both is indicated in the following appeal which Beck, who was to serve as temporary head of state, intended to address to the German people. It was one of several drafts considered by Beck and Goerdeler, and was designed to appeal to a nation that would still be under the influence of years of Nazi propaganda. Yet there speak from it the moral as well as the pragmatic reasons that impelled the men of July 20 to attempt the all but impossible.

> Germans:
>
> Monstrous things have taken place under our eyes in the years past. Against the advice of his experts, Hitler has unscrupulously sacrificed whole armies for his desire for glory, his presumption of power, his blasphemous delusion of being the chosen and inspired instrument of what he calls "providence."
>
> Not elected by the German people, but reaching supreme power by the worst of intrigues, he has created confusion by his demoniacal arts and lies, and by his incredible waste, which appeared to bring benefits to all, but which in reality has thrown the German people into tremendous debt. To maintain his power, he has established an unbridled reign of terror, destroying justice, banishing decency, mocking the divine commands of pure humanity, and destroying the happiness of millions.
>
> With deadly certainty, his mad contempt for all mankind had to result in catastrophe for our people. His self-bestowed generalship had to lead our brave sons, fathers, husbands, brothers into disaster. His bloody terror against defenseless people had to bring disgrace to the German name. Lawlessness, forced consciences, crimes, and corruption are what he enthroned in our fatherland, which before had always been proud of its justice and decency. Truth and honesty (ideals to which even the smallest of nations considers it education's greatest task to raise their children) are penalized and persecuted. Thus public as well as private life is threatened by mortal poison.
>
> But that must not be; we must not continue on that course! The lives and efforts of our men, women, and children must not be further

abused for such ends. We would not be worthy of our fathers, and our children would despise us, if we did not have the courage to do everything in our power, and that truly means everything, to ward off this fearful danger and to regain our self-respect.

To this end, having examined our conscience before God, we have assumed executive power. Our brave armed forces will guarantee security and order. The police will do their duty.

Let every public official follow but the law and his conscience, let him do his job to the best of his true knowledge. Let everyone help, in discipline and confidence. Put new hope into your daily tasks. Help each other! Let your tortured souls be calm and confident again!

Without hatred, we will attempt the act of domestic conciliation. With dignity, we will attempt that of foreign conciliation. Our first task will be to purge the war of its debasements, and to put a stop to the disastrous destruction of human life, and of cultural and economic treasure behind the fronts. We all know that we are not masters over war and peace. In firm trust in our incomparable armed forces, in confident faith in the tasks which God has given to man, we wish to sacrifice everything to defend the fatherland and to restore a just and true order, to live once more in respect of the divine commandments, to live in decency and truth, and for honor and freedom!

Rudolf Pechel, *Deutscher Widerstand* (Erlenbach-Zurich, 1947), pp. 305–306.

# JULY 20, THE AFTERMATH

Many people—perhaps as many as 5000—died as a result of the failure of July 20. Some committed suicide, others were shot, hanged from butchers' hooks, or tortured to death. (A special film of some executions was made to be shown to Hitler.) The following three documents give some small idea of the fate of these men. The first is a standard letter to the surviving family. The second is from Himmler's confidential speech to party leaders in Posen. The third is a bill for an execution, sent to the victim's family. It dates from an earlier case, that against a popular German cartoonist put to death for his frank expression of anti-Nazi sentiments; many similar bills then went to the survivors of the men of July 20.

OFFICE OF THE CHIEF PROSECUTOR     *Berlin W. 9*
AT THE PEOPLE'S COURT            *Bellevue St. 15*

*File No. OJ 6/44 Top Secret*          *Tel: 21 83 41*
*(Please give this number in your reply.)*     *October 25, 1944*
Baroness von Thüngen
(1) Berlin-Charlottenburg 9
Alemannen Avenue 6

The People's Court of the Greater German Reich has sentenced the former Lieutenant General von Thüngen[9] to death for sedition and treason.

The sentence has been carried out on October 24.

An announcement of his death is not permitted.

By order
[Signature illegible]

Hans Royce, ed., 20. *Juli 1944* (Third edition, Bonn, 1961), p. 223.

. . . The graves were dug so quickly that Herr Olbricht and other gentlemen were buried with their knight's crosses.[10] They were dug out again the next day, and there was a little checking on just who was who. I then gave the order to burn the corpses and to disperse the ashes over the fields. We do not want the least memory of these people, nor of those who are being executed now—not in the shape of graves, not in that of some other memorial. Reich Marshal Göring was entirely right when he said: Over the fields is much too decent, drop them over the sewage dumps. . . .

"Rede Himmlers vor den Gauleitern am 3. August 1944," *Vierteljahreshefte für Zeitgeschichte*, p. 382.

[9] All defendants holding military rank were deprived of that rank before being tried.

[10] Himmler is speaking about the first group of conspirators to be executed. They were shot at the war ministry in Berlin immediately after the failure of the coup had become apparent. General Olbricht had been deputy commander of the reserve army.

*PROSECUTOR'S OFFICE AT THE PEOPLE'S COURT*

File No. *4 J 777/44*
District Attorney's Office
*Statement of Costs in the Case Against Erich Knauf*

| | |
|---|---:|
| *Fee, according to Pars. 49 and 52 of the penal code, for death penalty* | 300.— |
| *Postal fees, according to Par. 71,2 of penal code* | 1.84 |
| *Fee, according to Par. 72,6 for court-appointed defense attorney, Counselor Ahlsdorff, Berlin-Lichterfelde-East, Gärtner St. 10A* | 81.60 |
| *Fee for prison stay, April 6 to May 2, 1944* | 44.— |
| *Costs of carrying out the penalty: Execution of sentence* | 158.18 |
| *Add postage for mailing the bill* | .12 |
| Total | 585.74 |

Payment must be made by the heirs of Erich Knauf, c. o. Mrs. Erna Knauf, Berlin-Tempelhof, Manfred von Richthofen St. 13, or Gilbert and Mach, Attorneys.

Royce, *20. Juli 1944*, p. 222.


# MAY GOD HAVE MERCY . . .

Among those arrested, tried, and executed that summer was Count Ulrich Wilhelm Schwerin von Schwanenfeld (1902–1944), army intelligence officer, country squire, and one of the earliest of the anti-Hitler conspirators. His last will and testament contained a passage which shall provide this book's last lines as well:

. . . *I further request that on that spot of the gravel pit of my Sartowitz forest where those murdered in the late fall of 1939 rest, there be placed, as soon as circumstances permit, a very tall wooden cross, made of oak, bearing the following inscription:*

HERE REST 1400 TO 1500 CHRISTIANS AND JEWS
MAY GOD HAVE MERCY ON THEIR SOULS
AND ON THEIR MURDERERS

Gollwitzer, *Du hast mich heimgesucht,* pp. 102–103.

# ACKNOWLEDGMENTS

Several people have provided advice and information of great value to this book. Special thanks are due to Michael Liggett, Peter Merkl, and Harry Steinhauer, all at the University of California at Santa Barbara, and to Robert P. Fenyo, history editor at Prentice-Hall. Two fellowships supplied the ingredient without which no book can be written, time. One came from the John Simon Guggenheim Memorial Foundation, the other from the Humanities Institute of the University of California. Both are appreciated more than this brief passage can indicate. Considerably more than routine gratitude, too, is owed to the place where much of the work on this volume was undertaken, the Hoover Institution on War, Revolution, and Peace at Stanford. It is unique, of course, in its resources on the period and topic, but it is equally without peer in the competence and kindliness of its staff. If it might not have appeared affected to do so, this book would have been dedicated to the Hoover Institution, that best of all possible libraries.

Help also was extended, and very much appreciated, by the Bundesarchiv in Koblenz, and by the Institute of Contemporary History in London. A number of authors and publishers, finally, have graciously agreed to permit the quotation of copyrighted material. They are: Bayerischer Schulbuch-Verlag, Munich, for Günter Schönbrunn, *Weltkriege und Revolutionen*; Bertelsmann Sachbuchverlag, Gütersloh, for Bert Honolka, *Die Kreuzelschreiber*, and Gerhard Schoenberner, *Wir haben es gesehen*; Bundeszentrale für politische Bildung, Bonn, for "Letzte Briefe aus Stalingrad," and Hans Royce, *20. Juli 1944*; The Clarendon Press, Oxford, for Samuel Dumas and K. O. Vedel-Peterson, *Losses of Life Caused by War*; Daily Express, London, for David Lloyd George, "I Talked to Hitler"; Walter de Gruyter, Berlin, for Friedrich Zipfel, *Kirchenkampf in Deutschland 1933–1945*; Deutsche Verlags-Anstalt, Stuttgart, for *Hitlers Zweites Buch*, Rudolf Höss, *Kommandant* in *Auschwitz*, and Melita Maschmann, *Fazit*; Doubleday and Company, New York, and A. P. Watt & Son, London, for *An Ambassador of Peace, Lord D'Abernon's Diary*; Europa Verlag, Vienna, for Hermann Langbein, . . . *wir haben es getan*; S. Fischer, Frankfurt, for Erika Mann, ed., *Thomas Mann, Briefe 1937–1947* (© Katja Mann), and Harry Pross, *Die Zerstörung der deutschen Politik*; Gütersloher Verlagshaus Gerd Mohn, Gütersloh, for Joachim Beckmann, *Kirchliches Jahrbuch für die Evangelische Kirche in Deutschland 1933–1944*; Karl H. Henssel Verlag, Berlin, for Helmuth James Graf von Moltke, *Letzte Briefe aus dem Gefängnis Tegel*; Chr. Kaiser Verlag, Munich, and Macmillan, New York, for Dietrich Bonhoeffer, *Widerstand und Ergebung*; Chr. Kaiser and Pantheon Books, New York, for Helmut Gollwitzer, Käthe Kuhn, and Reinhold Schneider, *Du hast mich heimgesucht bei Nacht*; Dr. Ruth Liepman, Zurich, for Inge Scholl, *Die weisse Rose* (© Inge Aicher–Scholl); Limes Verlag, Wiesbaden, for Gottfried Benn, *Ausgewählte Briefe*; Hermann Luchterhand Verlag, Neuwied/Berlin, for Heinz Boberach, *Meldungen aus dem Reich*; Gebr. Mann Verlag, Berlin, for Paul Ortwin Rave, *Kunstdiktatur im Dritten Reich*; Musterschmidt Verlag, Göttingen, for Walter Hubatsch, *Hindenburg und der Staat*; Bishop Dr. Johann Neuhäusler, for his *Kreuz and Hakenkreuz*; Nymphenburger Verlagshandlung, Munich, for Hans Müller, *Katholische Kirche und Nationalsozialismus*; Eugen Rentsch Verlag, Erlenbach-Zurich, for Rudolf Pechel, *Deutscher Widerstand*; Seewald Verlag, Stuttgart, for Henry Picker, *Hitlers Tischgespräche im Führerhauptquartier 1941–1942*; C. A. Starke Verlag, Limburg-Lahn, for Arnold Freiherr von Vietinghoff-Riesch, *Letzter Herr auf Neschwitz*; University of Chicago Press, Chicago, for Milton Mayer, *They Thought They Were Free*; Rainer Wunderlich Verlag Hermann Leins, Tübingen, for Marie Baum, *Leuchtende Spur*, and Walter and Hans Bähr, *Kriegsbriefe gefallener Studenten 1939–1945*; Wydawnictwo Prawnicze, Warsaw, for Stanisław Piotrowski, *Dziennik Hansa Franka*; and Paul Zsolnay Verlag, Vienna, for Erich Ebermayer, *Denn heute gehört uns Deutschland*. The author is indebted to all of them, for no selection really was replaceable.